ENGAGING COMMUNITY
HEARTS, MINDS, AND SPIRIT

ENGAGING COMMUNITY HEARTS, MINDS, AND SPIRIT

leadership for a sustainable world

Barbara A. Coe

ISBN: 1548005940
ISBN 13: 9781548005948

Contents

Acknowledgments

Many teachers have guided me in research and practice of community development and environmental work, and to each, I am most grateful. They are too numerous to include all by name here, but in particular, I want to thank the following people:

- My dear friend, boss, and mentor, the late William F. Gibbons, who demonstrated what an enlightened leader is, as well as demonstrating many technical aspects of planning for sustainable development
- Tom Walther and Robert and Rosalind Fritz, from whom I learned about the creative process and structural dynamics, the foundation for creating anything
- Dr. Robert Gates, professor emeritus, who guided and supported me in my dissertation research
- World Learning and the US Agency for International Development (USAID), for support of the project Communities Engaged in Social and Economic Development of Albania (CESEDA), and the managers who supported and guided me in my role as Chief of Party for that project
- The wonderful CESEDA team: Lead Coordinator Elona Boce and Field Coordinators Lumtor Vrapi, Brunilda Dapi, Kleidor

Rustemi, Suela Bejleri, Ornela Gjika, Dritan Sinakoli, Elton Jorgji, and Nexhmije Byku

- My dear friend, author Donna Caterina, who gave me constant moral support and also sound ideas for my writing

Last, but by no means least, I wish to extend my profound gratitude to my late husband, Dr. David K. Coe, who inspired and encouraged me to continue to study and to complete the PhD, for being my dearest friend and my soul mate during all the years we were together.

Combating Global Climate Change and Achieving Sustainable Development

Our world is in a mess right now, thanks to armed conflicts; horrific acts of violence; poverty, famine, starvation, and disease; and environmental destruction, much of it attributed to global climate change. All are connected; none can be addressed alone. To address these issues, scores of international organizations, governments, program donors, experts, practitioners and local communities have taken on both climate change and sustainable development. Despite intense and widespread effort, however, progress is much too slow and too limited. This book offers a new approach to help these organizations and their leaders, along with local community leaders, plan, design, sponsor, and guide efforts to achieve greater success. It describes how enlightened leaders, using a new, open focus framework that is grounded in structural dynamics, significantly improve success in combating global climate change and fostering sustainable development.

Among the most noteworthy international efforts are the Paris Climate Accord of December 2015 and the United Nations Development Programme (UNDP) (2017) Sustainable Development Goals put forth in 2015. The first of these, the Paris Climate Accord, is an agreement in which 195 countries adopted the first universal, legally binding global climate agreement. The agreement sets forth an action plan to limit global warming to less than two degrees Celsius (EU 2015). The second is UNDP's (2017) call to action to end poverty, protect the planet, and ensure that all people enjoy peace and prosperity. After extensive consultation with many other organizations, UNDP made its list of seventeen Sustainable Development Goals the keystone of its new agenda, adding climate change, economic inequality, innovation, sustainable consumption, peace and justice, and other priorities to the previous Millennium Development Goals. UNDP is charged with helping to implement the goals in 170 countries and territories.

As UNDP notes in its online introduction to the goals, "The goals are interconnected—often the key to success in one will involve tackling issues more commonly associated with another." Global climate change can be addressed by achieving sustainable development goals.

Even the most powerful world leaders seem unable to restrain continued degradation, however. Despite an abundance of intention, activity, agreements, and plans, global climate change and social and economic problems continue virtually unabated. Even if temporarily halted, problems often return with greater force. Implementing sustainable development goals requires substantial institutional and individual behavioral change. Because of the complexity of the environment in which these goals must be implemented, which requires the support and participation of myriad stakeholders at every level and also myriad policy decisions and actions, implementing sustainable development goals is the most difficult challenge. Technical issues are minor compared to the implementation challenge itself, which is generally not well recognized or understood.

To a great extent, success hinges on efforts at the local community level, those sponsored by other organizations and donors as well as those initiated locally. Local economic and social distress underlies much of global climate change and other environmental degradation. As noted primatologist and sustainable development activist Jane Goodall (2017) said in a recent interview, "Unless we do something to improve the lives of the people, unless we do something about the crippling poverty, where you have to cut the trees down to try and grow food or make some money with charcoal, conservation won't work. We've got to work with the local people, have them as our partners." As a result of this recognition, Goodall reoriented her organization's conservation programs to include economic development as well. This twofold approach, if it were adopted widely, could be a primary antidote to global climate change as well as other environmental issues. As such, achieving sustainable development goals is critical for both relieving human suffering and supporting the basis for human life.

Sustainable development goals can be addressed at the community level, even if central governments are not interested. As Michael R. Bloomberg (2017), a media tycoon and former mayor of New York City, said recently, American cities would continue to enact climate policies, no matter what the US federal government decided to do. The same can apply to governments worldwide. However, partnerships among international organizations, all levels of government, nongovernmental organizations (NGOs), businesses, and local communities, all working together toward common goals, *with the best available tools*, can achieve much more.

Implementing policies to combat climate change and achieve sustainable development goals at any level is exceedingly challenging. New approaches to implementation are necessary if climate change is to be reversed and sustainable development goals achieved. Efforts to engage a plethora of community members and organizations, all with their own agendas, operating principles, points of view, and leaders, must be supported and nurtured. In an arena where no one organization or leader has authority over the others, leadership approaches that work in individual organizations are ineffective. This arena requires a much more open, focused, inclusive, and collaborative approach to leadership. With such a new approach, international organizations, government agencies, NGOs, donors, practitioners, educators, and others who promote, sponsor, and guide efforts toward these aims, as well as local community leaders, could profoundly improve implementation success.

Some writers say that what is needed is "political will" (Mumo 2016). However, how does political will develop? It results from engagement within appropriate structures. Research into successful implementation in a complex community structure has shown that leaders achieve success when they use an approach specifically tailored to this arena (Coe 1986, 1987, 1988, 1991). The resulting "open focus framework" includes three factors to engage and mobilize others successfully: linking communication, collaborative vision, and evocative leadership. Following subsequent research and application, the approach was refined to include the creative process, grounded in principles of structural dynamics, which explains whether communities progress or oscillate (Coe

2001, 2013; Fritz 1989, 1996). The process includes four implementation steps:

- Engaging Community Hearts: Envisioning the Future
- Engaging Community Minds: Illuminating the Current Reality
- Engaging Community Spirit: Mobilizing Action and Sustaining Progress
- Completing and Celebrating Wins

The approach has been applied in various development projects.

Leaders who use this approach are able to engage the hearts, minds, and spirit of communities. They engage the hearts of community members when they tap into their aspirations and visions for the desired future of their communities. They engage their minds when they help them see objectively the whole of reality relative to their desired future, so they know what situation and barriers they face and what assets they have at hand. They also engage the spirit of communities—the essence, the character that defines the uniqueness of each community and gives it meaning. In this way, they spur people to engage not only willingly but passionately. They also cultivate expanded leadership, which is crucial to success in this complicated endeavor. The most successful are enlightened leaders, those who have exceptional maturity, an egoless commitment to the desired future rather than to their own personal rewards, and the discipline to keep progressing toward the desired future in the face of challenges. They can be role models for other leaders. Those who are genuinely interested in achieving sustainable development goals can use the practices of the open focus framework and the creative process to build awareness and to cultivate exceptional leadership skills.

Enlightened leaders may be found in government, in local and international NGOs, and in the business community, or they may be unaffiliated community members. They may or may not be formal leaders or the most visible ones.

This book describes application of the framework to a two-year project called Communities Engaged in Social and Economic Development of Albania (CESEDA). The project succeeded well beyond expectations: the fifty communities involved, which had never before engaged in any self-help activities, created fifty-eight major improvements in their communities and continued, after the end of the project, to use the process to make additional improvements.

A similar approach, grounded in structural dynamics, was used effectively in several other, very different places to foster sustainable development. One of the first was in Uganda. Assisted by Robert Fritz and Peter Senge, the leaders of the Uganda Rural Development and Training Programme (URDT) have sustained progress for more than two decades. From understanding how to generate and sustain action toward a desired future, the community leaders created a thriving organization that helps dozens of surrounding villages create sustainable development. As a result, URDT has been acknowledged at local, national, and international levels and has received numerous awards, including the 2003 Certificate of Recognition for exemplary environmental management and practices by the National Environment Management Authority and the 2006 Best Practice Award by the European Union Uganda Commission Civil Society capacity-building program, among many others (URDT 2017).

In Vietnam, the Vietnam-Sweden Forestry Cooperation Programme of 1996–99 used the creative process and structural dynamics as the foundation for a four-year sustainable agriculture and forestry development project. Swedforest, a Swedish consulting firm, began by training Swedish consultants and Vietnamese ministry staff in the process. Led by Jerker Thunberg, the team worked with communities in four provinces to produce exceptional results (Coe 1995; Thunberg, pers. comm., 2004). Only a few other cases of use by communities of the approach have been well documented; however, myriad organizations have used the approach to improve their results remarkably.

This approach has been introduced to many groups in both the United States and internationally to achieve results well beyond the typical ones. It has the potential to improve success. While the process may not overcome all social, economic, and environmental strife, it can make a significant difference in achieving sustainable development goals and combating global climate change. Where social problems and violence stem from exclusion and people's search for belonging, this inclusive and collaborative approach could provide a new pathway for many of the dispossessed.

ENLIGHTENED LEADERSHIP

Enlightened leaders, using the tools of the open focus framework, are both open and focused. They are, first of all, open to and focused on the good of the community, not on their personal rewards, while at the same time understanding enlightened self-interest, which recognizes that a socially, economically, and environmentally sustainable community benefits everyone. They are open to possibilities and focused upon a vision of a desired future. They don't discount goals as being unrealistic or impossible to create. They are also open to recognizing exactly what exists currently, not denying it, distorting it, or discarding knowledge of reality as too painful to face.

By exhibiting open hearts, minds, and spirit, these leaders invoke the same within the community in order to foster development of a shared vision. They trust in the goodwill of people, having confidence that most people are essentially well-meaning; they renounce an attitude of suspicion and prejudice that so often dooms community efforts before they begin. With this outlook, they are open to leadership by others, and they actively work to expand leadership capacity. They don't see leadership as a zero-sum game; rather, it's one in which all can win together. They understand that an undertaking as challenging as sustainable development requires the creativity, efforts, and leadership of many leaders. These leaders recognize that while success cannot be guaranteed, without a new approach, failure probably can be.

Open focus leadership relies upon "linking communication" to bring people together in a collaborative mode and support them in their efforts (Coe 1986). Linking communication includes two aspects: mechanisms for inclusion and knowledge dissemination; and attitudes and practices that inspire participation. This stimulates the community members to see possibilities and to become actively involved and invested in working with others to create the environment and opportunities that truly matter to them—despite what donors and outside developers might think is important.

Leaders are guided by the need to secure the community's collaborative vision as well. Only when people focus on a vision reflecting their own genuinely desired end results are they likely to mobilize and to sustain their activity. The process, which strives to engage all community members who wish to be involved, encourages a sense of ownership and caring for the community as a whole. When people come to know each other at a personal level and see each other as human beings with similar needs and problems, they are able to work together toward common aims.

Achieving sustainable development will require the leadership of many people working together toward the desired future, rather than at cross-purposes. Thus, these leaders are open to and deliberately cultivate and build the leadership capacity of others, helping them embrace and hone open focus leadership principles and practices. By example, they evoke enlightened leadership of others.

The approach is grounded in the creative process, the process used to create anything, and in the principles of structural dynamics that show how an underlying foundation guides action in every realm, including in human behavior (Fritz 1989, 1996). Although the creative process is well known in the arts and the sciences, it is not yet widely known as a foundation for community development. It can significantly help to mobilize communities and enable them to stay focused while taking and sustaining action toward their desired future. When leaders consciously use this process and convey this ability to the many people responsible for carrying out the necessary actions, they improve communities' ability to succeed. Understanding why the process makes the difference between success and failure and how to develop open focus leadership enables leaders to cultivate its use and to disseminate it.

EVOLUTION OF THE APPROACH

This book grew out of my realization, while I was working in a regional planning agency, that many plans don't achieve their goals or are never even implemented. Seeing that prevailing hypotheses for this failure were insufficient impelled me to research underlying explanations through both formal research and my work as a practitioner with many different communities in many different countries. My initial study of a complex public-private organization for my doctoral dissertation revealed factors of implementation success and failure and resulted in the open focus framework for success in the multifaceted community arena (Coe 1986).

In 1987, after learning about the application of structural dynamics to human systems and behavior, I revised the framework to incorporate this powerful new understanding (Coe 2001; Fritz 1989, 1996). More recently, exploration of Shambhala Buddhist thought has further deepened my understanding of enlightened leadership. Over the years, I used the revised process in working with communities, groups, administrators, professors, business leaders, and students in the United States, Armenia, Albania, Bosnia and Herzegovina, Georgia, Rwanda, Jordan, and Sri Lanka, and I presented it at conferences in various countries. Many participants embraced this approach; many have shown how it enhanced their success. Examples provided in the book come from many of these and from other practitioners using these practices.

This open focus approach to leadership is a radical shift from the problem-focused one commonly used to promote such aims as achieving sustainable development and combating global climate change. Although some specialists in community development claim that communities act only in a crisis, evidence and experience show that action of emergency has limited longevity, whereas positive passion—not problems—is what promotes sustained action. In fact, when presented with dire warnings, people often feel powerless to affect the situation and then want to hide from the reality. Nothing illustrates this more vividly than the widespread failure to act in response to warnings about global climate change.

Open focus leaders are drawn to ideas for community improvement, not prodded by fear of negative consequences. Although they are clear about the reality of the problems, they stay focused on the promises and possibilities, and they foster progress toward attainment of goals. They are more interested in achieving something positive than in destroying something they abhor. They are creators, not reactors.

Creating sustainable community development, a long-term proposition, is very different from simply working to eliminate problems. It requires working with multiple, diverse stakeholders and a shift in attitudes, expectations, and outcomes. Although learning the skill requires practice, and adoption and application will not be instantaneous, once the open focus approach to leadership is understood and applied, it can radically alter the future for many communities and thus for the world.

BOOK STRUCTURE

The following chapters show why a new leadership approach is needed and how open focus leadership can advance sustainable community development:

Chapter 2, "What Doesn't Work and Why," offers a fundamental explanation for the lack of sufficient progress toward combating climate change and achieving widespread sustainable development. Experts, stressing the unique characteristics of each situation, usually offer complicated explanations for why communities fail to achieve the results they seek. However, this chapter describes a common basis: lack of understanding and attention to two fundamental structures, the community structure and a mobilizing structure. These two structures explain and could have predicted most failed attempts to foster sustainable development (Coe 2008, 2013; Fritz 1996). The chapter provides a brief analysis of several implementation failures, from relatively minor ones to some with severe ramifications.

Chapter 3, "Enlightened Leadership for Successful Implementation," provides an overview of the open focus approach to leadership in the arena of community development. In this dynamic, inherently unstable, networked, multisector arena with myriad participants moving in and out of the process (often unpredictably), the top-down, authoritarian approach that may be effective in individual organizations is not applicable. Enlightened leaders understand both the limitations and the opportunities of this arena and how to work with them. These leaders are open to possibilities and to the reality, whatever it may be, and are focused on a vision for the desired future. In imparting this skill to others, they encourage them to lead as well. They engage the hearts, minds, and spirit of communities so as to evoke and sustain enthusiastic participation. Subsequent chapters describe the four steps of the process and how enlightened leaders use them.

Chapter 4, "Engaging Community Hearts: Envisioning the Future," shows how these leaders engage community hearts by helping to discover the community's values, vision for the desired future, and priorities—the first step in the four-step process. They guide people to find shared aspirations, identify goals that are mutually compatible, and, when necessary, guide them to a higher level of aspiration that encompasses seemingly different aims. By encouraging people to tap into their passions and pursue the future they genuinely desire, they engage the hearts of communities. Communities feel empowered by recognizing their heartfelt desires, starting to imagine possibilities, and envisioning the future they want.

Chapter 5, "Engaging Community Minds: Illuminating the Reality," shows how these leaders don't ignore existing conditions but guide communities to a clear, objective, shared understanding and articulation of the current reality, relative to the vision. It includes the status, available resources, and actual challenges. Because people often inadvertently or even deliberately distort reality and rely upon beliefs and assumptions, these leaders help to clarify what is real and what can and cannot be known. They demonstrate that admitting when they don't know what they don't know is not a crime and that being able to predict the future has great limits. Because communities can tailor actions appropriately only if they know both where they want to go and where they are, leaders who can guide them to this understanding are essential.

Chapter 6, "Engaging Community Spirit: Mobilizing Action and Sustaining Progress," describes the most critical element of the process—mobilizing action and sustaining progress over the long term. Enlightened leaders know that people are likely to act only when they are energized and galvanized at a deep and abiding level, when the desired future expresses the spirit of the community.

To accomplish anything, people must act. As Joel Barker (1985) has said, "Vision without action is merely a dream. Action without vision just passes the time. Vision with action can change the world." This chapter describes how enlightened leaders foster action without stifling creativity. They understand how action is taken and sustained, even when challenges arise. They approach action as an experiment, observe what happens, and compare interim results with the vision.

When working toward sustainable development, by keeping both the vision and the current state in mind, communities can see whether the actions lead toward the desired future. If the actions seem to be ineffective, they can then test other actions. Simple guidelines can help assure that the actions are on track.

These leaders know that forgetting or misconstruing either the vision or the reality can impede or prevent progress, so staying in touch with the impelling force is crucial. To assure continuous advancement, they help people stay focused on both the desired future and the current state. To achieve this, they remind the community of their vision for the future, while at the same time adjusting the view of the current situation as it changes over time.

In the fourth and final step of the implementation process, leaders work with people to bring projects to closure and then to acknowledge and celebrate wins. They realize that all involved benefit from noticing and feeling proud of their efforts and achievements. Celebration can take many forms, but it is essential. The chapter describes some of the successful, although sometimes rudimentary, celebrations that prompted renewed focus on the community and its development.

Chapter 7, "Accelerating Progress to a Sustainable Future," shows how next steps can lead to greater success. Previous chapters will have shown how and why the usual problem-focused approach to achieving sustainable development goals fails, how progress is often thwarted or reversed, and how open focus leadership can advance sustainable development. Now the critical question is, how can this approach be disseminated and used by those responsible for assuring a future that supports the needs and goals of people and the environment worldwide? The chapter suggests some access points and some influential organizations that could sponsor demonstration projects or elicit understanding and action. It challenges readers to be open to new ideas. As one participant in this process astutely observed, "This is a completely different way of thinking!" If widespread sustainable development is to be achieved, it is likely to require "a necessary revolution," as Peter Senge (2008) argues in his book of that title. It will be a revolution in thinking and organizing. Enlightened leadership, grounded in the open focus framework and the creative process, is a starting point for such a revolution.

2

What Doesn't Work and Why

People around the world are attempting to combat global climate change and achieve sustainable development goals. International nongovernmental organizations (NGOs), national and local governments, community groups, and local NGOs develop vision statements, establish indicators, and prepare plans. They disseminate information about how to stimulate good development through good governance, wise resource use, healthy environments, alternative energy and transportation, and wise land-development patterns. Increasingly, businesses and business organizations see that sustainable development helps their bottom line. These are all encouraging signs.

Yet these efforts are failing to change the course. Implementation of goals in this kind of complex, highly networked, multi-stakeholder arena is the greatest challenge to combating global climate change and achieving sustainable development. Communities often run out of steam before progressing very far along the path or are distracted by other demands. Some reverse direction and trash their own efforts toward sustainable development in favor of expedient development, hawked by arguments that valuing the environment will somehow destroy jobs and economies. Clearly, implementation requires a different approach.

A common but crucial missing link is an understanding of the role of structure in implementation and how to work with it. This includes both the structure of the community itself, which demands a tailored leadership approach, and a mobilizing structure that guides action either toward the goals or into forward/backward oscillation that thwarts success. Understanding and working effectively with these two types of structure is essential for progressing toward sustainable community development.

STRUCTURE MATTERS

Why is the structure of communities so important as to demand a special kind of leadership approach? Fostering sustainable development requires the participation and support of myriad organizations and individuals with different priorities, values, intentions, resources, and levels of influence. It requires that the community be brought together to collaborate around some common themes. It requires commitment and action over a long period.

The structure of communities, whether geographic communities or communities of interest, makes this extremely challenging. As figure 2.1 (below) shows, a community is a complex network of nodes of individuals and individuals representing organizations that are loosely connected in a plethora of multisector combinations. Not all of the individuals and organizations are connected with all others; some participants connect with some stakeholders, some with others. Because some of the connections may be temporary while others are permanent, the community is complex and inherently unstable. Participation is inconsistent; some organizations and people participate some of the time, while others participate at other times. Individuals often represent an entire organization, itself often complex, that must be brought along if progress is to be made. In this arena, individuals and issues come and go, often unpredictably, so that the character, makeup, and future of the arena are always changing and uncertain.

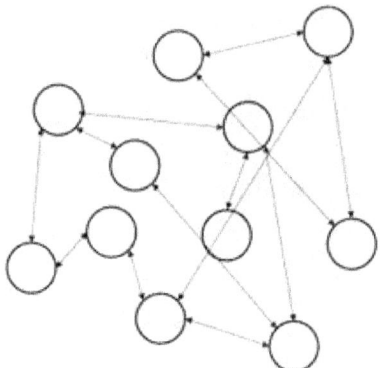

Typical Community Structure

Figure 2.1. Organizations and individuals are linked in various ways.

This community structure requires a very different approach from that of a single organization, in which lines of communication and authority are relatively clear, participation is relatively stable, and the people in charge set the expectations. In the community structure, no one person or organization is in charge or in control. Generally, both participation and compliance are voluntary. The arena often seems chaotic, like a garbage can of stuff in which "organizations make choices without consistent shared goals" (Cohen, March, and Olsen 1972, 1). Ordinary organizational leadership strategies and approaches that assume stability and control are not applicable here.

In this arena, in which people must voluntarily participate or may even have veto power or power of the purse, leaders must capture the collective power that is needed to move forward vigorously.

To do so, vision and energy must come from the community at large, not from a leader presenting a vision for others to follow nor from the outside. When leaders are ignorant of or closed to the visions and wishes of the community, they cannot engage the hearts, minds, and spirit of that community.

Furthermore, if leaders engage only selected members of the community, rather than all who wish to be included, they lose the latent energy and action available in that community. This may also foster conflict and resistance. When they fail to create adequate communication channels, community members lack information to learn about opportunities for participation. When they are blind to the feelings and needs of participants or would-be participants and fail to communicate with them in a supportive way, they also fail to stir interest in participation or even foster active opposition.

Leaders who focus on the kudos or material rewards they themselves can reap, rather than on the community's well-being, have great difficulty engaging others. Those who are authoritarian or controlling in their approach tend to get strong resistance (Coe 1986). Even when leaders recognize the futility of the direct approach and attempt to sell others on their ideas, community members recognize and resist the manipulation. When leaders refuse to consider others' ideas and remain wedded to their own perspective, they fail to engage others. When they are closed to leadership by others who are willing, holding it closely to themselves, they encounter passivity and inertia.

Many community leaders commonly rely upon traditional modes of hierarchical leadership. They focus more on attaining or maintaining power than on the actual well-being of the community. Because they lack interest in sharing or fostering the leadership of others, they tend to clamp down harshly on any opposition, in an act of fear. They consider others' ideas to be irrelevant unless they can use them for their own benefit. Without leadership suited to the complex structure, sustainable development (or any development that will broadly benefit the population) is unlikely to be achieved.

For example, in one public-private partnership for downtown development, a dynamic, visionary, and forceful president had ideas for more sustainable development (Coe 1986). Despite his community vision, community members didn't trust his motives. After seeing him forcefully push his agenda, they voted down some important initiatives. His dominance precluded input or leadership roles by other stakeholders. His failure to engage a broad spectrum of the community or to treat others in the organization with humility limited community support and engagement. After he was replaced by a more low-key, collaborative leader, the organization was able to create a thriving, exciting, and livable downtown.

Leadership to achieve sustainable development goals requires a very different approach, one that is open to the arena, to the actors in the mix, to the facts of the situation, and perhaps most importantly, to possibilities and priorities. When leadership is not fitted to the arena, apathy or unproductive conflict usually result. Even leaders who are committed to the community good can limit progress toward sustainable community development if they lack understanding of the unique community structure. The chances of success are reduced when a leader, uncertain of how to foster collaboration and enthusiastic engagement, instead relies upon power-focused leadership approaches.

MOBILIZING STRUCTURE

A second kind of structure—a mobilizing structure—underlies all action (Fritz 1989, 1996). This foundation guides a community either forward toward its aspirations or repeatedly forward and then backward in an oscillating pattern, a pattern that is all too familiar to community development actors (fig. 2.2.). Although the phenomenon of underlying structure is well understood in the arts and sciences, its application to human behavior, and specifically to sustainable community development, is still relatively unknown. Yet it is instrumental. Without an appropriate underlying structure, forward movement is stymied.

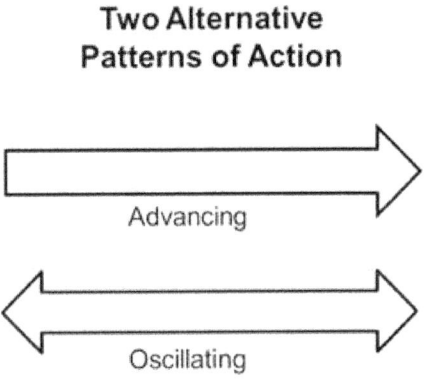

Two Alternative Patterns of Action

Advancing

Oscillating

Source: Fritz 1989, 1996

Figure 2.2. Action moves forward, making progress, or back and forth.

DUNES AND TIDES

Dunes and tides illustrate how structure underlies these two patterns of movement—advancement and oscillation—in the physical realm of nature. The dunes on the southern Brazilian coastline move inexorably farther and farther inland, impelled by the underlying structure composed of the relationship among the tides, winds, waves, ocean currents, and storms, which interact to sculpt the sand formations (Braga 2015. Unaware or unthinking officials and developers try to stop the dunes. They establish new urban areas in front of or on top of these dynamic landforms. Nevertheless, the sands keep coming. As a result, in many coastal communities, sand covers sidewalks and gardens and curves around the sides of buildings. Bulldozers busily work to take the sand away in an un-ending effort to reclaim urban sites, but at what cost? Moreover, with what likelihood of success? The dunes will return, reshaping the coastal landforms as they have done for thousands of years. Foolish people have thought they could ignore the natural move-ment of the dunes, but as always, the structure has the last word. Sustainable development cannot be achieved without considering the structure.

We can contrast the pattern of movement of dunes with that of tides and waves. The tides and waves come in, and then they go out again, forward and backward, governed by the relationship among elements such as drift currents, rip currents, winds, sea-level rise, and many other components (Braga 2015). The structural founda-tion supports their movement in an oscillating pattern. Sometimes the waves are higher and more intense than at other times, depend-ing on the winds. Sometimes they move farther inland. Inevitably, they will reverse and recede because of the structural foundation. Because of the structure, the dunes move forward, and the tides and waves move forward and then backward.

Similarly, structure underlies the behavior of humans and hu-man systems (Fritz 1989, 1996). This structure consists of thinking, beliefs, and positions of the people and organizations involved.

The structure supports either forward movement or oscillation. A structure designed to create forward movement is a simple one: it consists of a vision or desired end result and also a clear picture of the current status. The difference between the two generates energy for action. In community development, when a community has a shared vision of its desired future and simultaneously a clear understanding of the current situation relevant to that future, the tension between the two motivates the community to move toward its desired future (fig. 2.3).

Effective Sustainable Development Pattern

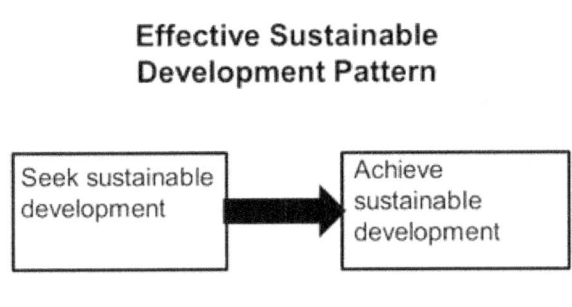

Source: Fritz 1989, 1996

Figure 2.3. Advancing sustainable development pattern.

As shown in figure 2.4 below, the tension stimulates action toward a goal. When people focus on what they want while also clearly understanding the current state relative to that goal, the difference between the two automatically establishes a phenomenon known as "structural tension." This structural tension has a natural tendency to resolve, similar to the tension of a stretched rubber band. The tendency of this tension to resolve propels forward movement.

How Structural Tension
Stimulates Action

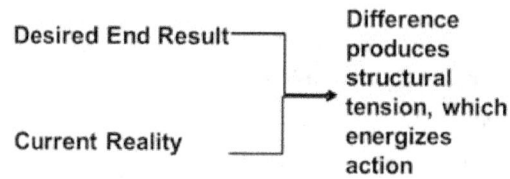

Desired End Result

Current Reality

Difference
produces
structural
tension, which
energizes
action

Source: Fritz 1989, 1996

Figure 2.4. Structural Tension stimulates action.

However, when a community has a conflicting force, such as a faction opposing the proposed goal, this creates a second tension-resolution system. When two competing tension systems exist at the same time, the energy will shift from one to the other and produce oscillation (fig. 2.5). In other words, in this complex tension-resolution system, as the tension increases in one system and decreases in the other, the community shifts the focus from one to another ad infinitum (or until giving up on the goal). This is, unfortunately, a common pattern in community development.

Common Structural Conflict in Development

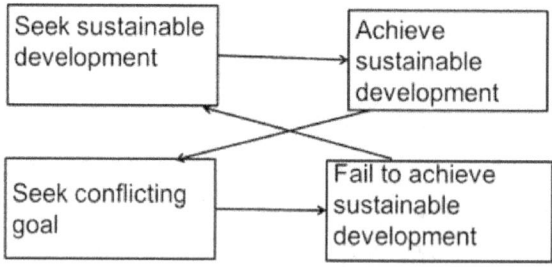

Figure 2.5. Community oscillates from one goal to another.

Just as the dunes and tides have different structural foundations guiding their patterns of movement, people also have two different patterns of behavior: advancement and oscillation (Fritz 1989, 1996). With a simple structure in place, one supporting a pattern of advancement toward a goal, the person or group takes action until achieving the goal or deciding to discontinue. In a complex structure, one characterized by conflicting goals (thus designed to produce oscillation), the person or group takes action toward a goal, then away from it to the conflicting one, then toward the goal, and then away again, either never attaining the goal or attaining it and then losing it. This is structural conflict, conflict driven by the underlying structure. The underlying structure leads either to a pattern of forward movement toward a goal or to oscillation, toward and away from the goal, back and forth.

These two alternative patterns of action—advancement and oscillation—are commonly seen in attempts to combat climate change or to achieve sustainable development goals. The structure underlies these patterns. Because it can either energize forward action or cause it to reverse and stall, the structure is a major factor in the limited success thus far in fostering sustainable community development. When not moving forward toward their desired futures, communities become locked in patterns of oscillation.

EXAMPLES

This structural conflict explains a common situation in which the goals of some developers who wish to develop land are at odds with those of conservationists who want to preserve an area without regard for other desires. In this situation, each of the groups has a different tension-resolution system. As shown in figure 2.6, the two systems conflict with each other, producing a pattern of oscillation in which the developers seek to move forward toward development, while the conservationists seek to move in the opposite direction. The pattern is back and forth as tension increases and then decreases in each of the two tension-resolution systems. This pattern will continue unabated unless one side completely overpowers the other, which is not beneficial either to long-term sustainability or to community relations (Coe 2013).

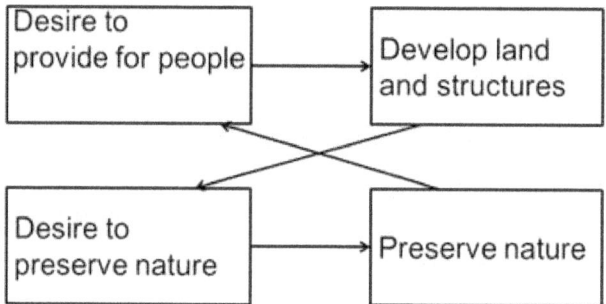

Figure 2.6. Conflicting goals lead to oscillation.

Structural conflict also occurs when some community groups are focused on short-term benefits, while others are focused on long-term values (fig. 2.7). For example, some stakeholders may be committed to creating immediate jobs, while others may be focused on conservation and sustainable development with no concern for the need for development. The community will continue in an oscillating pattern unless ways can be found to bring disparate groups together around a shared vision that accommodates seemingly diverse desires.

Oscillation Between Goal of Sustainable Development and Goal of Short-term Gain

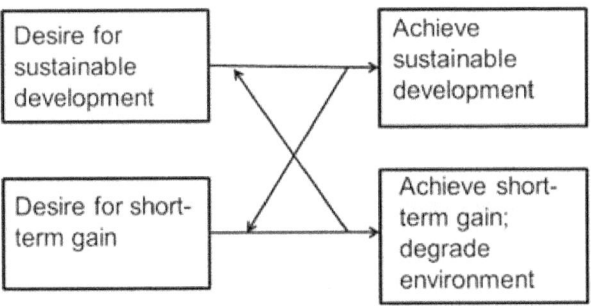

Figure 2.7. Sustainable development requires a long-term perspective.

STRUCTURAL CONFLICTS FROM BRAZIL TO THE UNITED STATES

Myriad efforts toward sustainable community development are sty-mied by structural conflicts. For example, since the early 1970s in Brazil, the Jaguaruna, Santa Caterina, coastline has shifted from small farming and fishing communities to summer beach towns. These communities witnessed the change from a seasonal influx of small numbers of summer residents, big-city families who braved bad roads to reach paradisiacal beaches, to the now continually growing communities that depend economically upon seasonal tourism (Braga 2015; Gruber et al. 2013). Jaguaruna is a classic case because considerable urban and economic development pressures generate an array of environmental, economic, and social conflicts in which state and local governments frequently neglect, or even sometimes approve, new public and private developments, all in the name of progress.

In 2000, in an attempt to protect the environment, the Brazilian federal government established a marine and coastal protected area

(APA) in the area of Jaguaruna and sixteen neighboring municipalities (Braga 2015; Gruber et al. 2013). However, people and local governments fail to comply with this and other laws and regulations that exist to control or guide land-use decisions in line with the environmental reality. A person builds a house without a permit, or the local government approves a big development because it is purported to bring in significant tax revenue. These decisions create enormous management challenges, including problems created when there is a lack of sanitation systems to manage the black-water drainage, which then gets channeled into the sea; the depletion of pre-Columbian archaeological earthworks known as sambaqui, hills of deposits of seashells and other artifacts; or civil works that cross dunes in the APA, altering the natural dynamic cycling process that normally protects neighboring land uses and ecosystems. In the wake of such initiatives comes political pressure to install public utilities and other services. Thus, environmental degradation grows while remediation and mitigation of the conflicts become more complex and expensive. Although many of the stakeholders in Jaguaruna are attempting to find common ground toward a more environmentally and economically healthy Jaguaruna, these structural conflicts among the decision makers hamper planning for sustainability (fig. 2.8).

Structural Conflict in Jaguaruna, Brazil

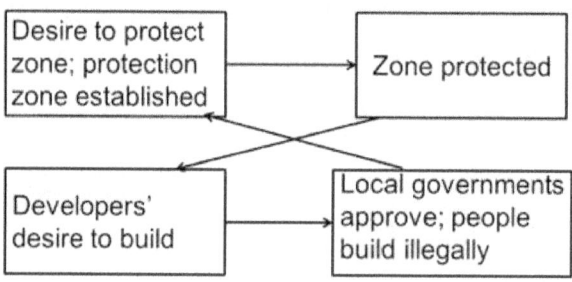

Figure 2.8. Structural conflict produces oscillation.

Another example, although much less dramatic, illustrates how oscillation can occur even when groups have a shared goal, if they become distracted by lesser goals (fig. 9). For example, when people disagree about what actions to take or about how to organize themselves, they tend to stop advancing together or they react to an external event and lose sight of the primary goal. In such cases, two tension-resolution systems develop, one that remains focused on the desired end result of sustainable development and another that becomes focused on other things and ignores the original purpose. The structural dynamics here produces a pattern of oscillation rather than advancement.

The Colorado Sustainability Project (CSP) in the United States shows how a group effort was thwarted by structural conflict when the group's focus shifted to a lesser goal. The project was intended to foster high-level decisions supporting statewide sustainable development. Initially, a leader who was inspired by participation in the Rio Conference in 1992 pulled together a group of proponents of environmental education and advocacy in the Denver-Boulder metro area. Volunteers designed, coordinated, and facilitated a Colorado Summit, intended to galvanize political will to produce policies for a sustainable Colorado. More than two hundred participants enthusiastically embraced the charge and formed task groups for research, communication, and other topics, with about twenty-five members actively involved. When the initial CSP steering committee disbanded, a new steering committee was formed, consisting of a representative of each task group.

However, the new steering committee shifted its focus to organizational issues and away from the primary aim of policy measures, thus creating a structural conflict (fig. 2.9). Although the group needed an organizational structure, when they ceased to focus on the participants' passion for sustainable development, energy dissipated. People dropped out, and task groups disintegrated. Although the group eventually formed a formal organization, it was short lived. This is a common structural conflict between ends and means. Attention shifted back and forth between the two, limiting progress. The group lost the mobilizing power of the vision. Had the goal of advancing policy to support a sustainable Colorado been kept clearly in mind as the primary goal, with the organizational decisions serving the major goal and the ends and means clearly illustrated, the group may have sustained the structural tension to continue to advance.

Structural Conflict:
Primary VS Lesser Aim

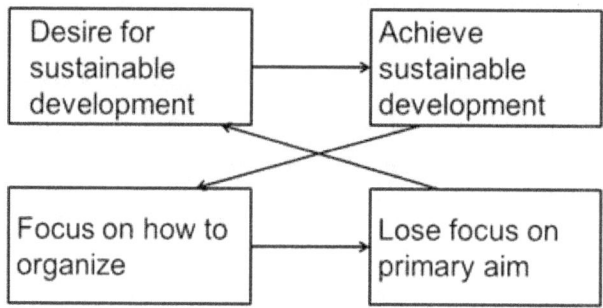

Figure 2.9. Shift of focus from sustainable development to organization form produced oscillation.

FOCUSING ON PROBLEMS LEADS IN CIRCLES

Structural dynamics underlying community action also precludes success when the focus is on a problem, as is common, rather than on the vision, desired results, or goal. A problem focus produces a circular pattern that usually ends with return of the problem or the emergence of a new problem. As the illustration below (fig. 2.10) shows, when the community focuses on eliminating a problem, the motivation for action is to get relief, not to create something. The process of simply taking action against a problem produces a sense of relief, causing community action to slacken and eventually stop. Although communities often act vigorously in a problem-driven emergency, once they achieve some relief, efforts tend to fizzle. The energy is not sustained. Thus, a problem focus, although appropriate for addressing crises in the short run, does not allow for sustained focus and action over the extended period necessary for sustainable development. It precludes the use of the powerful tension that the creative process affords.

Problem Focus Leads to Nothing

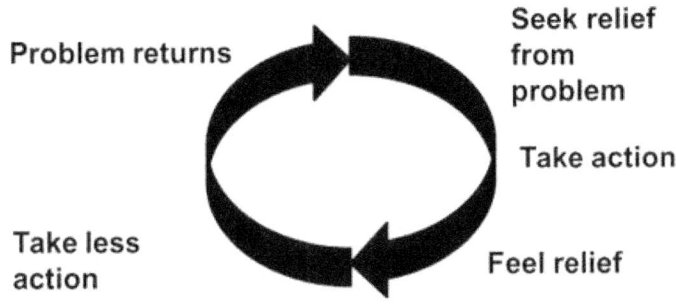

Figure 2.10. Seeking relief leads to less action
and often to return of the problem.

Many examples of the results of a problem focus, as differentiated from a vision focus, are readily available. One example is the city of Denver, Colorado, which was plagued by many gang-related murders in the late 1980s and early 1990s. The community mobilized and took action to combat this problem. The murder rate declined; however, a graph of homicides in the city shows a clear pattern of spikes in the murder rate in 1986, 1992, 2004, and 2015 (Phillips 2016). Each period of action was followed by a significant drop in the murder rate, which was then followed by another spike. This pattern is typical of a problem-focused approach, as differentiated from a vision-focused one that, while recognizing the problem, focuses on a desired result, an approach that potentially could have produced a very different outcome.

This discussion has shown how an underlying structure guides action in nature and by people and communities, propelling either a forward or an oscillating pattern. Sustainable community development efforts are rife with forward-backward oscillation, driven by structural conflicts resulting from differing goals among different stakeholders and with circular patterns that lead nowhere. When communities hold conflicting goals or have an unclear picture of reality, they oscillate rather than advance toward sustainable development goals. When they are driven by problems, rather than focused on a vision, they end up back where they began. Sustainable development goals cannot be achieved within a structure that is designed to produce oscillation or a circular pattern; achieving them requires a structure designed to support forward movement. Establishing such a structure can be difficult, given a plethora of actors with different views, but without a structure designed for success, the effort is futile.

Despite the many existing structural conflicts commonly seen in sustainable development efforts, all is not lost; communities need not continue with an either/or approach to development decisions that produce only oscillation. People need shelter, business, shopping, and recreation; locking up all natural environments denies these needs. At the same time, the natural environment is the foundation of life; its destruction by thoughtless and careless development can have devastating long-term consequences, both for the environment and for future development itself, as seen in Jaguaruna. Sustainable development enables the environment and social and economic development to complement each other. Efforts to achieve it can be designed to work with nature and with the two kinds of structure essential to success.

STRUCTURE FOR SUCCESS

Staying on the path toward achievement of sustainable community development goals requires that communities come together around shared visions for their future and take appropriate action, often for a prolonged period. Given a genuine desire for sustainable development and leaders who understand how to work with both the structure of the community and the structural underpinnings of human action, this can be done. With these in place, communities can sustain the action required to advance toward sustainable development naturally. This is the alternative to continued conflict and oscillation.

Any effort to lead communities toward sustainable development requires leaders who know how to guide the community forward. Enlightened leaders, using practices of open focus leadership, engage the hearts, minds, and spirit of the community. They work effectively with the community structure, building the necessary relationships and fostering commitment to shared goals and shared understanding of the current reality. They work with the mobilizing structure to help energize and mobilize communities and help them stay focused on the desired future for as long as necessary. The following chapters describe attributes of enlightened leaders and how they apply the open focus framework to the four steps leading toward implementation of sustainable development goals.

3

Enlightened Leadership for Successful Implementation

Successful implementation of goals in the complex, multi-stakeholder community environment is extremely challenging, particularly in regard to combating global climate change and fostering sustainable development. As our original research into successful goal implementation revealed, enlightened leaders in this endeavor understand how to work effectively with community and mobilizing structures to engage the hearts, minds, and spirit of communities and to evoke the leadership of others to help communities advance (Coe 1986). The research resulted in a framework called "open focus," an encompassing concept that included three essential elements: linking communication, collaborative vision, and evocative leadership. These elements are dynamic and symbiotic, occurring sometimes sequentially and sometimes simultaneously and building upon and enhancing the others. Continuing research and application led to refinements of the framework that was eventually informally tested in the 2004 Communities Engaged in Social and Economic Development of Albania (CESEDA) project (Coe 2008, 2013). Using these practices, successful leaders guided communities in four main implementation steps, which are described in subsequent chapters:

- Engaging Community Hearts: Envisioning the Future
- Engaging Community Minds: Illuminating Current Reality
- Engaging Community Spirit: Mobilizing Action and Sustaining Progress
- Completing and Celebrating Wins

OPEN FOCUS

Open focus is an attitude, a worldview, and a starting point for the leader and the community (Coe 1986). It suggests both an openness to and an understanding of the external environment and the complex and interlocking network of the community itself. Open focus requires that the various components of the community—individual structures and the political, technical, social, and economic environments—be viewed as pertinent to goal achievement. Leaders in this mode seek information and are open to learning from a variety of sources. They look forward to the long-term implications of trends, events, and actions. They understand the necessity of broad stakeholder involvement in all stages. They are flexible and understand the need to consider a wide range of alternatives presented, even from nontraditional and unexpected sources.

Communities working in this mode reflect a strong sense of mission and goals; they present a clear picture to the outside world. They focus and stay focused on where they want to go. Communities and their leadership are aware of and communicate clearly about resources available, and they are honest about limitations and weaknesses. They make efficient and effective use of human, financial, and other resources. Because they have a clear focus, they do not automatically accept or reject new concepts or opportunities; they consider them in light of their ultimate aims. They are poised and ready to capitalize on trends and innovations while avoiding detrimental knee-jerk reactions.

Enlightened leaders engage the community to foster such an open focus stance. They offer vision, creativity, and a readiness to be on the front lines to help a community improve. They are willing to be visible and responsible, and they do not wait for someone else to take charge. At the same time, they are open to others' ideas and leadership. They stimulate community members' interest and encourage them to participate not only willingly but passionately.

These leaders feel empathy toward the experiences and limitations of others. They recognize that an individual's ego needs will persist and that people don't have perfect foresight. Rather than becoming frustrated or angry, these leaders are supportive; they mentor people to improve their capacity to use the tools that will help the community move forward. They understand that only when communities have both a shared vision for the future and a shared understanding of reality can they tailor actions to advance.

Enlightened, community-minded leaders may be found anywhere; sometimes they hold official positions of power in government, but very often, they do not. They are often informal leaders in communities or change agents from outside the community. Some of them may have acquired a desire and a talent early in life to be of service and to lead effectively; others may have learned through experience or conscious cultivation of an open focus view and practices through self-reflection, awareness, and skill building.

Enlightened leaders engage the hearts, minds, and spirit of communities using the three main elements of the open focus framework: linking communication, collaborative visioning, and evoking leadership.

LINKING COMMUNICATION

My research of successful implementation showed linking communication to be essential to achieving goals. Because no one entity in a community has control, relationships must be established and nurtured to bring stakeholders on board. Effective leaders use linking communication to engage communities fully and collaboratively. This has two aspects: First is the establishment of open, inclusive mechanisms to reach the community as a whole, including minority, marginalized, and often-excluded groups. The mechanisms are designed to spread accurate information widely and to assure transparency about meetings and decisions, so people understand the community plans and how they were developed.

Communication is two-way: networks move information throughout the community and help build trust and interest, setting the stage to develop common goals. Enlightened leaders go beyond mere transparency, seeking information from all who are willing and able to provide it; they know that local knowledge is invaluable. Communication links expand the structure to a network of networks. Extensive communication broadens understanding of the facts and the values, concerns, needs, and behaviors of stakeholders.

Networks include all stakeholders who have relevance to the situation, not only formal leaders and institutions but also informal society. "Community engagement" is not simply about involving so-called civil society organizations (CSOs); it also requires the involvement of members of the community at large, whether organized or not. Simply having representatives of specific groups is insufficient unless those representatives have been democratically selected by the groups they purport to represent.

Communication mechanisms are tailored to the environment and circumstances. In the original research, one-on-one meetings, group meetings, and semi-social functions, published announcements and media were common. In Albania's poor rural communities, however, word of mouth was the primary mode, along with posters in prominent spots such as health clinics or schools. Meetings were generally group meetings, to assure that everyone had the same information and to avoid an indication of favoritism or deceit. In the current environment, media is often used, but it must be used very carefully so as not to spread false information and foment mistrust.

The second aspect of linking communication is supportive communication, communication that honors and respects all others. These leaders know that an atmosphere of trust and respect—prerequisites for developing shared values, mission, and goals—is essential to the implementation of any plan. They exhibit empathic openness to others and to their participation and ideas. They consider all people of equal value, and they enable all to be honest about their needs and views. They are not defensive or resistant to ideas that may differ from their own; nor do they employ intimidation, force, or manipulation. They are supportive of everyone who is interested in participating, and they encourage all to be involved in ways that suit them. They use *focused* listening techniques, including being present with the speaker—being mindfully, respectfully, and genuinely interested in what is being said and in the speaker's experience.

Enlightened leaders also are sure to give recognition and credit to those who contribute. They do not hoard the limelight. By engaging community members in this way, enlightened leaders help to stimulate and mobilize the community commitment necessary for progress.

COLLABORATIVE VISIONING

Secondly, research showed that an inspiring, shared vision is essential to successful implementation. Establishing a pattern that supports achievement of development goals requires collaboration by many participants in setting and implementing appropriate policies and practices, and it requires a prolonged effort over a considerable time span. In this environment, where no one person or organization has control, and participation in implementation is largely voluntary, people will only make an effort to achieve goals about which they care deeply. Communities must find a shared vision for their desired future or some aspects of it. It must be that of the community, not that of a leader or of an outsider. That shared vision must be consistent with the community's spirit and nature.

Collaboration in developing a vision also brings additional resources that improve that vision: technical and local knowledge, evaluation, assistance with leadership, improved communication, and shared workload. Through collaboration, communities have access to more ideas and inventions; through synergism, they gain expanded visions. They have greater understanding of the situation and of likely outcomes of various strategies. Furthermore, collaboration helps to establish the necessary linkages between formulation and implementation. When those who must implement goals are involved in their formulation, they own the goals. When they aren't involved, they are much less likely to be inspired to follow through. A mutual sense of direction sets the stage for forward motion.

Decisions about visions need not necessarily be unanimous. Consensus—that is, the agreement of stakeholders to support a vision—is sufficient. Alternatively, they can agree to support different aspects of the desired future one at a time. Where communities have disparate views, they can often find overarching visions to incorporate various desired end results through collaboration.

Collaboration, although essential to implementation success, is not simple. Participants generally promote their individual views and interests. Some people may feel threatened by the process, especially if they see it as diluting their own power. Collaboration takes more time than does goal setting by a leader or a few people. However, the time is well spent, since participation is key to successful implementation in this arena; without it, success is unlikely.

Enlightened leaders see a collaborative vision as the doorway to the hearts, minds, and spirit of communities. It's also essential to community commitment and sustained focus. The development of trust, respect, and understanding through linking communication and an attitude of openness to others and their ideas helps set the stage for effective collaboration. The research showed that leaders who effectively guide communities forward put the community first; they have a passion to be of service to the community (Coe 1986). Because they are committed to the good of the community and not to their own self-interest or to using power, influence, and projects for personal benefit, they inspire others to become involved. They are in sharp contrast to power-hungry, dictatorial, corrupt, or ruthless leaders—who are not likely to foster collaboration.

EVOKING LEADERSHIP

The research showed the importance of expanded leadership to successful goal implementation. Achieving development goals requires the leadership of many people working collectively toward the desired future. Enlightened leaders are not only open to but deliberately evoke, cultivate, and build the leadership capacity of others, helping them embrace and hone open focus principles and practices. This may be the quality that sets these leaders apart, more than any other. This is in sharp contrast to some worldwide examples of contemporary leaders who guide transformational movements only to revert afterward to the power-grabbing practices of their predecessors.

Enlightened leaders who evoke the leadership of others may be visionary or facilitative. In any case, they don't hold leadership closely; they don't consider themselves to be the only or even the primary leaders. Rather, they recognize that the efforts of many leaders will be required if sustainable development goals are to be achieved. They have a sense of aspiration and commitment but do not attempt to control. They are open to others' ideas, visions, and points of view. They encourage others' creativity and independence. They operate from a sense of possibilities, not limits. They inspire in others a commitment to lofty goals and a willingness to follow those goals through to success. They tap the greatness in others, support their best, and refuse to support their weaknesses. They take whatever role is necessary to assure that goals are met, including taking the visible lead when called for but getting out of the way when that is more appropriate—even if the influence of others transcends their own.

By example, these leaders demonstrate to emerging leaders their commitment both to the community above their own personal gains and to open focus practices. They convey the importance of clarity about the desired future and the related reality and how to guide others to find that clarity. They demonstrate open communication, the ability to communicate clearly and supportively, rather than defensively. They establish workable communication links that others can emulate. Most importantly, they show other leaders how to maintain the energizing tension, without which even the best-conceived and most well-intentioned community efforts are likely to die. Leadership expands geometrically. As some leaders evoke open focus leadership of others, those leaders in turn are inspired to pass it along.

One leader working in sustainable development who exhibits these attributes is Professor Nelson Gruber, Vice-Director of the Geosciences Department of the Federal University of Rio Grande do Sul, in Porto Alegre, Brazil. While leading analyses of the geological considerations, he demonstrates his passion for sustainable development that preserves the integrity of the seacoast of southern Brazil while also accommodating the needs of people. He is open to learning all he can about the situation and how to achieve sustainable development. He exhibits no desire for personal gain or fame but frequently puts his own needs aside at considerable personal cost. He supports and encourages leadership by others from all sectors. His approach keeps the possibility of sustainable development in this region alive and advancing.

Likewise, the late William F. Gibbons, who was Development Planning Director for the Four Corners Regional Planning Commission, a multistate economic development agency led by the governors of the States of Arizona, Colorado, New Mexico, and Utah, plus later Nevada, exhibited similar attributes. He was committed to the mission and goals of the organization and the region it served rather than to personal rewards; he was respectful of others and open to their ideas and input; he nurtured the leadership capacity of staff and provided ample opportunities for them to take leadership roles.

Enlightened leaders also understand how to work with the mobilizing structure. By using the creative process, in which open focus leadership is grounded, these leaders are able to help communities mobilize and sustain actions toward their desire future and to impart this skill to others (Fritz 1989, 1996). Using open focus practices, enlightened leaders using the open focus framework (fig. 3.1) effectively guide communities through the four implementation steps:

- Engaging Community Hearts: Envisioning the Future
- Engaging Community Minds: Illuminating Current Reality
- Engaging Community Spirit: Mobilizing Action and Sustaining Progress
- Completing and Celebrating Wins

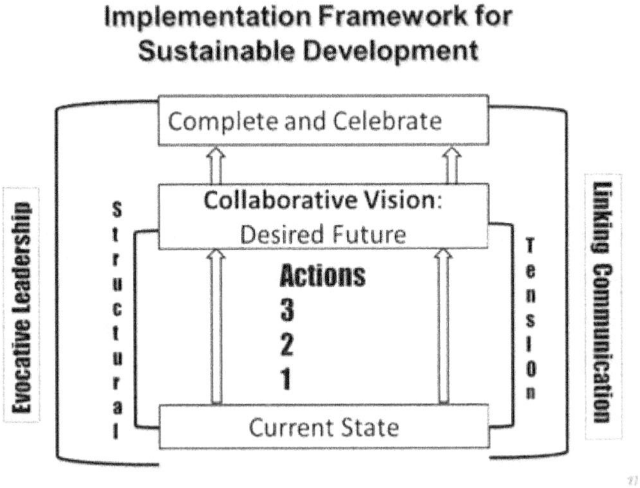

Implementation Framework for Sustainable Development

Figure 3.1. Enlightened leaders use the three elements of the open focus framework to carry out the four steps of the implementation process.

Each of these steps produces synergy. When people experience success in one stage, they become more energized, empowered, and eager to advance toward the future they seek.

STEP ONE
ENGAGING COMMUNITY HEARTS: ENVISIONING THE FUTURE

When communities focus upon a vision for a genuinely desired future—such as a sustainable community that serves the well-being of all of its inhabitants—their hearts become engaged. When people focus on something they really want and start to see the possibility of its realization, they tend to become inspired. Coupled with subsequent steps, their vision impels and guides action.

A genuinely desired vision is neither a problem to solve nor a means for reaching the desired future. It is not limited to what people might decide is possible, since no one knows for certain at the beginning what might be achieved. It is concrete enough for the community to recognize, even though it may not be measurable in numeric terms. It is not intended to benefit only a favored few but to benefit the community broadly. Although people, especially those in poor communities, may never have considered the possibility of a better future, when their imaginations soar, they are transformed.

Every significant change starts with a heartfelt dream. Enlightened leaders help the community tap into those heartfelt dreams of the community.

STEP TWO
ENGAGING COMMUNITY MINDS: ILLUMINATING CURRENT REALITY

To achieve their goals, communities must also have a clear and objective picture of the current status, resources, and barriers to success. Without knowing the current status of the community relative to its goals, they cannot know what steps to take. Even so, this step is often ignored in community planning, often with ridiculous or dire consequences. This step not only enables wise planning but also establishes a motivating tension that actually helps the community advance (Fritz 1989, 1996).

Leaders in an open focus mode are open to recognizing and acknowledging the current reality, however good, bad, or ugly it may be. The current reality includes the current state relative to the desired future, the assets available, and any real barriers to advancing toward the vision. Leaders ask probing questions to help community members attain clarity about and accept that the current reality is what it is, without exaggeration or other distortions. These leaders know that even if the current reality is unpleasant, the community must have an accurate and shared understanding of it in order to advance and achieve its goals.

STEP THREE
ENGAGING COMMUNITY SPIRIT: MOBILIZING ACTION AND SUSTAINING PROGRESS

The spirit of the community is both its essence and its motivating force. When this spirit is captured in its vision and its understanding of itself, the community is mobilized to take action to become more of what it can be, to create its desired future.

Communities can only advance when they take action and sustain it until they reach their desired results. Since many different pathways may lead to the desired future, successful communities approach action as an experiment, observe what happens, and compare interim results with the vision. If the actions seem to be ineffective, they can then test other actions.

This dynamic environment may not resemble the past; entirely new actions may be required. Leaders must establish mechanisms for gathering ideas and comments and must engage others in decision making and action. In the open focus mode, they are open to many possible ways to advance without undue attachment to either their own or traditional approaches. They don't deny or veto suggestions instinctively or habitually; they listen attentively and consider the ideas seriously. They demonstrate that all contributions are valued, even when not all ideas can be used. Action is encouraged without stifling creativity. In this way, hearts, minds, and spirit are further engaged.

SUSTAINING ACTION

Action will mean nothing unless communities stay focused and move forward. Since achieving sustainable development goals is a most complex endeavor, requiring many different actions by many different people and organizations, it requires a commitment to staying focused on the desired future while taking action, even in the face of challenges and real barriers. When communities commit to a clearly defined future and at the same time accurately perceive the relevant current reality, they automatically establish a remarkable phenomenon called structural tension, a phenomenon that is well known and applied in the arts, sciences, and technology but that is still relatively unknown for its application to community development (Fritz 1989, 1996). This structural tension is the engine for forward motion because the natural tendency of structural tension is to resolve itself.

Enlightened leaders facilitate progress by helping communities use this indispensable tool. They help communities advance toward the desired future by engaging community hearts, minds, and spirit and cultivating use of the creative process. They do not react and respond to every problem and issue; they know that a reactionary approach reduces the likelihood of real progress. They help to sustain focus by reminding the community of the vision and the reality as it is, including problems and barriers, and they do not hide the truth from themselves or others. They know that keeping both the vision for the desired future and the current status clearly in mind will enable the community to choose actions that make sense. This will also help community leaders track progress, and most importantly, use the natural tension to keep them moving forward. Enlightened leaders also help the community expand participation. Communicating the difference between the desired future and the current state reveals next steps and suggests how others can participate and also help to lead.

STEP FOUR
COMPLETING AND CELEBRATING WINS

Completing and celebrating are two often-overlooked but integral parts of the process to achieve goals. Sustainable community development is always a work in progress; it's more of a direction than a place at which to arrive. Noting and celebrating progress toward sustainable development acknowledges the community for its commitment and effort. At the same time, this further energizes the next steps. This is especially critical when processes rely extensively upon voluntary action.

Completion can be difficult. Participants are sometimes unsure when a project is really complete, or they may be reluctant to end their activity, possibly leaving a void. However, this step is essential and can help to energize the community further.

Celebrations are usually proportional to the achievements; they can be as simple as words of praise for a task well done or as involved as inspiring in-house ceremonies or community-wide celebrations with food, music, and public speeches. Even if sometimes rudimentary, celebrations afford a visible illustration of the work a community does. They also prompt a renewed focus on community goals.

For example, in Albania, community festivals provided both a means for developing organizing skills and fun for the residents. One successful village festival to promote turkey sales for New Year's Day was continued in years following, providing increased income, reduced transportation costs (for sellers individually taking their turkeys to the city), and lively community events.

The range of possible ways communities can choose to celebrate themselves, their aspirations, and their successes is enormous. The point is that they do celebrate, taking advantage of the opportunity to acknowledge their effort and to inspire further advancement.

CONCLUSION

By engaging the hearts, minds, and spirit of communities, enlightened leaders can help communities achieve sustainable development goals. Achieving goals can be fraught with resistance and conflict in common current political environments in which so many actors think only about short-term profits or personal rewards.

Enlightened leaders put the community first; they do not seek personal fame or riches. They seek, rather, a healthful and productive life for all in the community. They use open focus practices—being open both to possibilities and to the current reality and to leadership by many others. Knowing that a problem focus is suited only to crises, they guide the community to focus on the long-term desired future.

These leaders are open to input and feedback and establish effective means to engage the community in all facets of the process that supports advancement toward goals. They treat actions as experiments, assessing what might need alteration to advance more readily. They show the community how to use the mobilizing, structural tension to set up a path of least resistance that helps the community move naturally toward its goals. They acknowledge and celebrate effort as well as both small and large victories. Not least, these leaders build capacity in the community to be clear and focused and to keep moving forward toward the desired future, even if it requires a long time.

The following chapters describe how enlightened leaders use open focus practices to carry out each of the four implementation steps to help communities achieve their goals. The chapters demonstrate the application of the framework to the CESEDA project to achieve unusual success. Project results illustrate the efficacy of this approach and its ability to mobilize communities. Most importantly, the communities continued afterward to use the tools for further community improvement.

Enlightened leaders begin with the first step in the implementation process: Engaging Community Hearts: Envisioning the Future.

4

Engaging Community Hearts: Envisioning the Future

The first step in the implementation process is engaging community hearts. When shared by many in the community, a compelling vision for the future can truly engage the hearts as well as the minds and spirit of the community. Although all steps in the process are required, this first one—a mental picture of a completed result—inspires the community to begin the process. Then, this picture must be kept in mind. The chapter describes how leaders overcome challenges to effective participation and help communities identify and focus on their vision. It offers some guidelines for carrying out this step. It then describes how the Communities Engaged in Social and Economic Development of Albania (CESEDA) project conducted this step.

As discussed earlier, achieving sustainable development goals requires participation by many people and organizations, appropriate policies and practices, and prolonged effort over a considerable time span. In less-developed or transitional communities, donors and implementers often rush in with their own ideas about what a community needs—without first consulting with the community. They doubt the ability of the local people to choose wisely.

However, attaining community commitment to the action required to realize sustainable development goals requires that the vision be a collaborative community vision, not that of only one or a few local leaders or outside agents. It must also reflect the community's nature. An inspiring vision that engages the hearts of the community will also more effectively mobilize community action.

Although people, especially those in poor communities, may never have considered the possibility of a better future, when their imaginations soar, they are transformed (Coe 1995). At the beginning of a big sustainable development project in Vietnam in 1995, when a change agent asked villagers about their dreams for the future, a man in a village lacking even water, sanitation, or electricity hesitated. After a moment's thought, he suddenly brightened and said, "My kids having a college education!" Whether this man's lofty dream was realized or not, it likely set the stage for his children or for future generations.

The complex community structure makes finding shared visions challenging; barriers will inevitably arise. Leaders need effective tools. Enlightened leaders first convey the power and necessity of clarity about the desired future and then help communities focus and stay focused on their visions. Enlightened leaders use the three open focus practices—linking communication, collaborative vision, and evocative leadership—to help communities discover their shared visions.

DISCOVERY PROCESS

Discovering the collaborative vision in a community requires candid and in-depth conversations, asking people to picture how they want their community to be. Because many people have never considered this question, the process can be painful at first. It is a matter of opening to the desire that lies dormant until permission is given to express it. As Charles Eisenstein (2013), author of *The More Beautiful World Our Hearts Know Is Possible*, discusses, it is not about creating a vision; it is about *receiving* a vision. These efforts are enhanced by using practices of open focus. But first, people must be involved and engaged.

LINKING COMMUNICATION

In this initial step, enlightened leaders use linking communication to engage communities fully and collaboratively. In the first of two aspects, they establish open, inclusive mechanisms to reach the community. They make sure to inform community members about the project and its processes. They conduct open, inclusive processes to seek information about values, aspirations, and visions of the community as a whole, including marginalized groups. They establish mechanisms to gather ideas and comments and engage others in decision making and action. Because misinformation and closely held information are two of the most destructive means to thwart community progress, they want to assure accuracy from the outset. In rural Albania, where citizens lacked access to electronic media or newspapers at the time, most information was shared and learned via word of mouth. One main message was that the project was inclusive. Open meetings assured transparency and wide dissemination of accurate information about meetings and decisions, so that people understood community plans and how they were developed. Leaders sought not only transparency but active participation by all who were willing and able.

The second aspect of linking communication, supportive communication, refers to the manner in which leaders communicate.

Therefore, in eliciting input, leaders exhibit empathetic openness to others and to their participation and ideas. Because they consider all people and their ideas of equal value, they are open to and respectful of all input. They actively seek and distribute information widely, even if it reveals flaws in the knowledge or performance of a leader or team. By engaging community members in this way, enlightened leaders build community trust and confidence to begin to mobilize the community commitment and energy necessary for progress.

The process of engaging people can take many different forms. In small communities, leaders may engage all who want to participate. In larger communities or when resources are very limited, the number of possible participants may be more limited. Various venues for assuring inclusivity are available. Some specialists have developed effective techniques for engaging a thousand participants or more at a time. For example, people meet in small groups; then the results of their discussions are consolidated. Some communities invite all who are interested to post elements of a desired future on a big board; coordinators then organize these elements into categories, which become the initial vision statements to be used in following steps. Although many group intervention methods are available, it is not our intent to present a comprehensive description; other resources describe various intervention methods in detail.

Whatever process is used for engaging people, leaders gather community groups and facilitate community discussion and decision making. They lead the community in open processes to discover shared values, aspirations, visions for the future, and priorities. They help them discover mutually compatible and supportable goals and desired end results or outcomes, using the practice of collaborative visioning.

COLLABORATIVE VISIONING

The leader helps community members discover a vision around which they can organize. Because communities must support goals and take substantive action if goals are to be achieved, the values, vision, and priorities must be their own and must be developed collaboratively by those members of the community who care to be involved. Because people commit to taking action and to following through when they care deeply, the vision must be heartfelt. Enlightened leaders engage community hearts by guiding members in identifying their deep aspirations.

As indicated earlier, achieving sustainable development requires many leaders to guide implementation of sustainable development goals. Therefore, enlightened leaders also evoke the leadership of others.

EVOKING LEADERSHIP

Enlightened leaders engage, evoke, and support the leadership of others in helping communities discover their visions. Because these leaders focus on achievement of community goals, they don't strive to be in the limelight or think about getting credit for achievements. To assure that the community can advance as effectively as possible, they strive to transmit leadership skills to as many willing and able community members as possible.

Community members may have a variety of goals for the community's future, and some of the goals may be considered incompatible. Sometimes leaders can help communities discover a higher level of aspiration that accommodates seemingly incompatible ends. For example, when development and a healthy environment are discussed, proponents of each often find that this is a false dichotomy. Both a healthy economy and a healthy environment are required if both are to thrive, and each depends upon the other. With this awareness, community groups can seek ways to achieve both desires simultaneously, rather than continuing to oppose each other. Other times, communities need to put aside their differences, find some shared elements of their desired future, and implement first one and then another of those elements.

Enlightened leaders understand and accept differences. They don't react; they simply acknowledge them. They don't seek unanimity on every goal but rather seek consensus on at least one or more that the community can commit to implementing. When communities disagree about which goal is most important, the leader helps them see that multiple goals can be achieved, one by one. Very often, when communities begin to work together to implement one of the goals, they begin to discover many shared ideas.

WHAT IS A MOBILIZING VISION?

A collaborative vision consists of desired end results or outcomes that are widely shared by the community. They reflect what the community wants to see in place, its desired future, or an aspect of it. To be mobilizing, the collaborative vision must express genuinely desired end results, not problems to solve, means to an end, or assumptions about how things should be. Desired end results must be specific and concrete enough to know when they are achieved, although not necessarily numerically measurable. They are rich and genuine, not small-minded. They are oriented to the good of the community, not to the benefit of only certain individuals or groups.

Leaders guide communities to structure workable desired end results that reflect their genuine aspirations with the aid of these guidelines.

DESIRED END RESULTS ARE NOT PROBLEMS TO SOLVE

Perhaps most importantly, the vision statements express what people want, not problems they wish to eliminate (Fritz 1989, 1996). Communities are inspired and committed to sustained action by true aspirations. As Thankyouocean.org reported in 2017, people advocating *for* the establishment of an ocean sanctuary off the coast of California succeeded, while groups repeatedly fighting *against* offshore oil drilling usually end up fighting the same fight again and again.

Starting with a vision of a desired end does not deny the existence of a problem. The problem is also kept fully in mind, as will be discussed in the next chapter. Community action is, however, often driven simply by a problem; attention is focused on eliminating something but without any vision of a desired result. A problem focus is appropriate in an emergency, when quick action is required. However, a problem focus is designed to achieve short-term results. It is not effective for achieving sustainable development goals. Although this difference may first appear to be simply semantics, it is much more. The community's focus of attention has the power to either inspire or discourage. Research shows that when people focus on problems, they tend to feel powerless and overwhelmed, rather than motivated (Coe 1997, 2008; Fritz 1989, 1996; Kretzmann and McKnight 1993; Senge 2008).

Structurally, a problem focus tends to lead to a circular pattern: people take action to try to eliminate a problem; as the pressure lessens, they take less action, and the problem returns (Fritz 1989, 1996).

When attracted by a vision instead of driven by a problem, communities take different actions. When drawn forward by a vision such as "community residents being safe," people concentrate on developing strategies for the long term, rather than simply getting rid of the immediate problem. This is essential if communities are to advance toward sustainable development, which requires a long-term continuous commitment. As posted on the Robert Fritz Inc. website (2015) regarding the Uganda Rural Development and Training Programme (URDT), "This effort is led by my long-time friend and colleague Mwalimu Musheshe who has brought the creative process to rural development and brought new levels of understanding and dramatic improvement when people place the power in their own hands through such things as structural tension. The URDT (Uganda Rural Development & Training Programme) is forging new ground for questions of development, not as aid imported by external forces which tends to make people less self-generating, not as problem solving which is one of the worst ways to address issues of development, but from within communities themselves, so people find the power of their own creative process." A vision focus is inspiring and empowering. Most importantly, it is mobilizing and can sustain action.

DESIRED END RESULTS ARE CONCRETE

Communities often set goals that are too vague to be implementable—"prosperity for everyone" or "good health for everyone" are typical examples. Although these are worthy aims, they must be operationalized more concretely to be useful mobilizers. Both prosperity and health can be defined more specifically: "Every community member has an adequate home and sufficient food for maintaining life" or "Every community member is healthy enough to conduct his or her daily activities." Communities use indicators to be even more explicit. Although desired end results need to be concrete enough for the community to recognize them when they achieve them, they don't necessarily need to be measurable in numeric terms. For example, communities in Albania focused on the desire for all-weather roads to enable them to get their agricultural products to market, their families to medical care, and their children to school. Through collaboration, the vision expands to incorporate additional aspects and eventually evolves into a vision that takes on a life of its own.

DESIRED END RESULTS ARE DESIRED ENDS, NOT COMPARISONS WITH THE CURRENT STATUS

Related to the need to be concrete about desired end results is the need to specifically characterize them so that they can be recognized when attained on their own. The use of comparative words such as *less/decreased* or *more/increased* is not simply a matter of form; it can actually limit a community's ability to focus and stay focused. Expressing their desire in comparative terms means that they will have to keep referring to the original state, just so they can gauge whether or not they are making progress. Also, since the vision of the desired future is the impetus for motivation, focusing on the comparative fails to capitalize on this powerful force.

DESIRED END RESULTS ARE END RESULTS, NOT A MEANS TO AN END

Communities often confuse means with ends. They often jump to perceived solutions and become attached to their favored solutions and closed to other alternatives. Desired end results must express the desired future, not the means for reaching that future. Commitment to action comes from imagining the desired future, so keeping the vision separate from the means enables continued focus while testing various ways to achieve the desired ends.

For example, the desire that Albanian communities initially expressed for health clinics in their communities was actually a means to an ultimate aim—accessible, high-quality health care. Clarifying the true desired end result revealed that improved transportation would serve this end better than health clinics in every tiny village, at the same time providing other benefits as well. In another instance, the community expressed the desire for a bridge over a sometimes-raging creek that often kept kids from attending school. Their focus on the outcome—kids getting to school—was what mobilized the community to build the bridge. When communities first identify the actual desired end result, they will be able to consider various options for action and select the best one.

DESIRED END RESULTS ARE DESIRED, NOT "SHOULD BES"

Sometimes communities confuse desired end results with ideas about what "should be," out of some sense of "rightness." For example, some people might have the sense that a community *should* have a park or a school or be clean. However, if people in the community don't really care about these things, they won't be motivated to act. Expat-led community projects in Albania and elsewhere often focus on community cleanup or other simple tasks. Residents comply—but not enthusiastically. Rather, they are energized by focusing on aspects of the future they genuinely want.

DESIRED END RESULTS MAY ENCOMPASS APPARENTLY CONFLICTING DESIRES

Sometimes communities express desired end results that may be or seem to be mutually incompatible. In some cases, overarching choices may encompass apparent contradictions under one umbrella. For example, sustainable development bridges an apparent dichotomy between development and nature conservation by envisioning a future that includes both protection of nature and the provision of people's needs—even if the means for achieving it is unknown at this stage.

If no overarching idea seems available to bridge diverse views, the community may identify some agreed-upon goals to address first. They can prioritize their desired end results, addressing first one and then others. Alternatively, they may decide to break into work groups to tackle several aspects simultaneously. After working together, members are likely to reach agreement more readily on various other goals. Conflict need not stop progress. Communities can nearly always find some shared goals to pursue together.

DESIRED END RESULTS MAY OR MAY NOT BE POSSIBLE

Desired end results are not limited to what people might define as possible. People want what they want, whether or not it is possible. In any event, no one knows for sure at the beginning what might be achieved. In Albania, when community members were asked what they wanted, their responses invariably concerned physical infrastructure. Many other development projects placed aspirations this large out of bounds, directing communities to be realistic and to engage only in such simple things as cleaning up trash or holding roundtables, thereby failing to tap into the spirit of the communities. CESEDA, on the other hand, encouraged communities to aim for their true aspirations and not to limit themselves. Many were surprised when the communities completed many improvements that previously had been considered far beyond community capacity—roads, a renovated school, a cemetery, even a sewage-disposal system—usually using their own labor.

When the vision expresses the community's true desired ends—not problems to solve, means to an end, or what "should be"—and is discovered through collaboration among interested community members, it sets the stage for the community to move forward vigorously toward its goals.

ENGAGING COMMUNITY HEARTS IN ALBANIA

The CESEDA project used the open focus framework from the outset and throughout the project. In the rural Albanian communities in which CESEDA worked, all interested members of the target communities could participate. Coordinators simply invited all community members to meetings where they learned about the process and decided upon priorities. Word of mouth quickly encouraged the congregation of other groups. Instead of outside donors or implementers or even government officials, community members were the ones who decided what their priorities should be.

Some projects built in Albania without community consultation had resulted in such debacles as school buildings with bathrooms but no running water, teachers, or desks. Some project implementers had engaged only formal leaders of the community, who are often more attuned to their own desires than to those of the community as a whole. As one amazed participant said to field coordinators of the CESEDA project, "No one ever asked us what we wanted before!"

Because organizations had generally conducted projects in Albania without input from the intended beneficiaries, communities were accustomed to having others provide aid without community effort. As a result, they were unaccustomed to participating. Field coordinators suggested that the "mentality" of community participants needed to be changed. They discovered that communities became energized when they were invited to participate in the process to identify and work toward what truly mattered to them. In doing so, these leaders were able to effect change in the attitudes of community members.

CESEDA coordinators used open focus practices throughout the process. The coordinators fostered openness to all who wished to participate. They used linking communication to assure that all who wished to be involved were informed and participating. They guided the decision-making process respectfully. They employed appropriate and effective techniques to find common ground among a diversity of participants, to foster accurate, shared understanding. Later, they helped participants stay focused.

As indicated above, the communication mechanism was mainly word of mouth and observation. In villages, not much happens that escapes attention. Open meetings that were often held outdoors in full view of everyone assured transparency. Wide dissemination of accurate information about meetings and decisions assured that people understood community plans and how they were developed. The coordinators exceeded mere transparency, actively seeking the participation of all who wished to be involved.

By their manner toward others, CESEDA coordinators demonstrated that all the contributions were valued, even though not all ideas could be used. They communicated in an open and supportive manner and exhibited empathy to others and an openness to their participation and ideas. They considered all people as equal participants. Because they were truly interested in the experiences and opinions of community members, they listened mindfully and respectfully. They were not defensive or resistant to ideas; they did not employ intimidation, force, or manipulation. They facilitated decisions and sought unanimity or consensus around choices.

Throughout the process, coordinators facilitated a collaborative decision-making process to ensure the participation of all who were interested and to help community members find agreement at each step. They encouraged community leaders to come forward. Many who did so were women who were eager to improve conditions for their families.

REPORT-CARD PROCESS

Initially, eight field coordinators, working in male/female teams of two, and a lead coordinator, all bright, young, knowledgeable Albanians, contacted local residents, sometimes education or health-clinic administrators. These local leaders provided information about the villages and helped to organize groups, which often met outside or in school buildings or clinics. Coordinators had little trouble gathering groups for the report-card process. Not much else was happening in the villages; this was the place to be. People seeing others participating often asked to contribute also. CESEDA tried to accommodate all those who wanted to be included, rather than selecting for participation only certain "leaders" or other people known by local officials, as is common in such projects. The intention was to dig deeply into the heart of the communities, to learn what people truly wanted and to build capacity for engagement and achievement as widely as possible. In this way, CESEDA was able to engage more than 10 percent of the project area's population who were eighteen years of age or older.

In the report-card process, coordinators invited participants to evaluate the community services they received (or often didn't receive). After participants identified which services they wanted to evaluate, they were asked to assign grades to each, using a typical report-card format. This process was instrumental in attracting people. People loved giving their opinions in this way. After all, expressing opinions about conditions was a privilege that had been denied people for decades but was no longer threatening.

However, the report card was only the first step. Lacking additional tools, the effort would likely have produced little except some feel-good effects by people who had given their opinions. To begin to mobilize action, the field coordinators then led discussions of priorities that most interested the participants. (fig.4.1.)

Figure 4.1. Hillside meeting.

FOCUS ON PRIORITIES

After completing the report-card process with each community group, the coordinators asked the groups which of the community services that they had evaluated was most important to them and a priority for improvement. The choices were most often infrastructure of some kind, usually roads or water systems, followed by facilities such as schools, health clinics, and others.

Community priorities were often ambitious infrastructure improvements, but unlike the common practice of quashing big goals as "unrealistic," CESEDA coordinators supported, rather than discouraged, the group's ambition. People want what they want, whether or not they think they can achieve it. When they were clear about what they wanted, the villagers usually found the necessary resources to achieve the priorities that mattered most to them.

After the groups selected their priorities, coordinators then asked them to describe how they would like the situation or service to be in the future. They helped the people start to think in terms of actual desired results, rather than simply focusing on problems (fig. 4.2). They guided them to see that focusing on a vision ("a road that is usable in all weather") rather than a problem ("getting rid of potholes in the road") was a more engaging and useful approach.

Figure 4.2. Albania planning.

Coordinators helped the groups focus on their desired ends ("education for our children") rather than a means to an end ("a school building"). Through collaboration, the visions expanded to incorporate additional aspects and evolved into broader and more concrete visions that seemed real, even before they were completed.

Coordinators used a deceptively simple action planning process based upon principles of structural dynamics, which explain and guide sustained action (Fritz 1989, 1996). When properly used, these tools help groups focus and stay focused on desired end results and priorities, rather than spinning wheels or getting off track altogether, as often happens in such efforts.

Simple charts clearly illustrated the dynamics. After participants discussed and achieved consensus about the first priority, the coordinators recorded the priority at the top of the chart, to assure that everyone had it in view (fig. 4.3). Putting the description of the chosen priority at the top of the chart clearly illustrated what the community was aiming for. Subsequent steps in the process, described in the following chapters, added additional information to the charts and provided a clear visual to help sustain focus and guide action.

Action Planning Chart

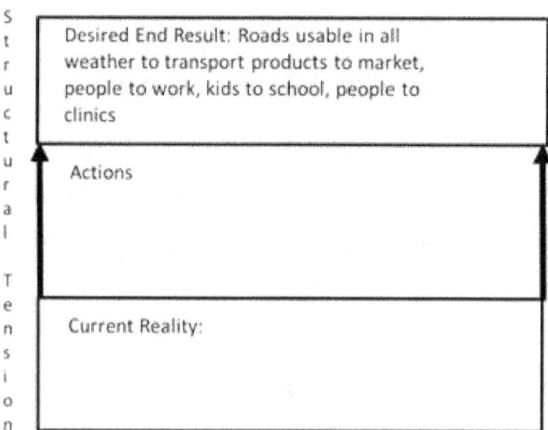

Figure 4.3. Coordinators used simple action planning chart to help people focus.

Initially, the CESEDA approach baffled the groups, who had no experience with planning and self-help. They were accustomed to bemoaning their situation while *others* decided what they needed. Expecting the usual approach, in which donors come bearing gifts, one participant asked, "So, what are you going to do for us?" The quick-thinking coordinator responded, "Have you ever had a meeting like this?" The man shook his head, so she continued, "*This* is what we are doing for you."

Soon, groups were joining in the process enthusiastically. Most importantly, when they started to define and to work toward their own aspirations, they became excited and enthusiastic. Their hearts were engaged.

Throughout the process, coordinators guided community members to focus and to stay focused on their genuinely desired end results and priorities, what they would like to have in their communities. Community leaders and members began to see that they had power to act on their own behalf and that they were not dependent upon others to do everything for them. They no longer wallowed in problems and self-pity. They did change their mentality. Because goals and priorities came from the community—not from outsiders who thought they knew what the community should want or what was possible or impossible—the groups were energized to pursue them.

BARRIERS TO PARTICIPATION

Barriers to participation can be daunting, especially in developing or transitional countries. Even in developed countries, leaders may encounter barriers such as "participation fatigue." Open focus practices help leaders address barriers skillfully.

HISTORICAL AND ECONOMIC BARRIERS

Engaging rural communities in Albania presented initial barriers that the coordinators worked to overcome in various ways. Social and economic conditions in Albania were dire, especially in rural areas (International Fund for Agricultural Development 2002). Under the highly restrictive communist dictatorship from 1944 to 1985, enormous resources went to building thousands of bunkers to protect the country from feared invasion by other countries, while real needs went unmet. A lack of decent roads for getting products to market, kids to school (usually on foot), or family members to clinics severely hampered hopes for social and economic development (fig. 4.4). Water and sanitary systems, education, and medical care were also all inadequate in most villages.

Figure 4.4. Transportation in Balaxhias.

After fifty years of living under this dictatorship, people lacked experience with participation or taking initiative. According to CESEDA local staff, during the dictatorship, residents were forbidden to sell anything on their own or even to tell anyone when the government store had no bread; they were all required to do "volunteer work" on their days off, which gave volunteerism a bad name for years afterward. At the same time, the dictatorship forbade community-initiated organizing or self-help activities. This experience produced a severe, long-term effect: citizens were wary of communicating or collaborating with the government or even with each other.

With such a history, it is no surprise that communities simply waited for government to provide for them. What was a surprise was the response of communities and the results they achieved once they began to think about what they wanted in their communities. Perhaps a lack of experience with community participation was actually a benefit, in that people were open to the process. They did not resist the efforts because of either preconceived notions about how processes should work or the participation fatigue experienced in countries with a strong practice of participation.

CULTURAL BARRIERS

The culture of Albania also presented noteworthy barriers. Cultural practices often forbid or inhibit women to meet in groups, to attend events that include men, or to go out in public at all. Because the women performed the majority of the work in villages while the men often talked, drank coffee or alcohol, and played board games, women had little time or opportunity to gather. They could only meet during lunchtime, early morning, or late afternoon. To assure the participation of women, field coordinators structured women-only meetings when necessary. They went where the women were and scheduled meetings at times when they could be available.

Additionally, rural residents were unaccustomed to being learners. This challenge was mitigated by first establishing a respectful working and partnership atmosphere and then moving on to the use of the tools. When some communities made progress, others saw what they were doing and were encouraged to try the process in their own communities.

LOGISTICS

Logistics presented a major challenge. For example, adequate meeting space was very limited, especially during the times that women could meet. Sometimes a school or a health clinic provided space (often, around an examination table). Because of cultural constraints, women usually could not meet in bars—often the only public space in a village. Culturally, people were unaccustomed and averse to meeting in each other's homes, as is done in many countries. Weather presented a barrier to meetings outdoors, although these became the norm in many villages. Finally, the abysmal infrastructure in rural Albania made mobility difficult and often impossible, while also suggesting that village priorities would be related to infrastructure. Although the government had paved many roads years before, given the abundant rain and complete lack of road maintenance for years, roads were riddled with huge potholes. Many streams lacked bridges. Meeting facilities were in short supply.

To overcome logistical barriers, coordinators drew upon their local village contacts and their own initiative to find meeting space in schools or health clinics. On one occasion, when an evening meeting was scheduled in a dilapidated school that lacked electricity, participants crowded around a pool table at a nearby bar (fig. 4.5). When no suitable indoor space was available, participants sat on a hillside or under a tree, with the ever-present flipchart in front of them, next to a shop or in the yard of a home on chairs collected from around the neighborhood, or clustered around a van onto which the flipchart was taped (fig. 4.6). Ingenuity and commitment enabled coordinators to find ways to achieve the task.

Figure 4.5. Participants clustered around a pool table.

Figure 4.6. Flip chart posted on van.

SUMMARY AND NEXT STEPS

Although sustainable development has generally been elusive, research and practice show that with enlightened leaders who engage the hearts, minds, and spirit of communities and with the right tools, communities can more readily achieve their goals. Coordinators in the Albania project used principles and practices of open focus throughout the project. From the beginning, they were open to all interested participants and their ideas and preferences. In this first step, they showed participants how to focus on their priorities. They demonstrated their commitment to their communities above their own personal goals. They understood that leadership had to come from the communities themselves. They took steps to find and cultivate participants willing and able to take on this role.

CESEDA coordinators served as facilitators rather than as formal community or governmental leaders in this project, but they cared deeply about helping communities in their country. From this basis, they fostered collaboration and built the capacity of informal leaders to engage others to create major community improvements. Although the communities started out being problem focused, they developed the skills needed to progress toward their desired future.

The process demonstrated that communities can be empowered, energized, and mobilized by imagining possibilities and envisioning their desired futures. When it comes from the community members who will be expected to implement actions, not from outside or even from a small number of leaders, the vision of the future—the desired end result—becomes the force that primes community action.

Although some writers claim a vision is all that is necessary to manifest results, research and experience show otherwise (Fritz 1989, 1996). More is needed. Namely, the vision must be thoroughly grounded in a clear understanding of the current reality relative to that vision.

The following chapter, "Engaging Community Minds: Illuminating Current Reality," turns to the second step in the process.

5

Engaging Community Minds: Illuminating Current Reality

As described earlier, the first step for successfully implementing sustainable development goals is to engage community hearts by eliciting a shared vision of the community's desired future. As indicated above, successful implementation requires that the vision be grounded in an accurate understanding of the reality relative to that vision (Fritz 1989, 1996). Not only does this assure that actions taken subsequently make sense, it also establishes an energizing tension that helps communities move forward toward their goals.

The current reality includes the current state relative to the desired future, the assets available, and any real barriers to advancing toward the vision. It can be characterized as fact versus other-than-fact. Strangely, this step is often overlooked in community planning. First of all, this understanding enables communities to take actions that make sense. Just as knowing the starting point is essential before planning a successful trip, so too must we know our current situation before taking action toward any goal. If developers and decision makers in Jaguaruna were clear about the reality of the movement of dunes, they could make better decisions about the location of urban development.

However, an even more important reason lies behind the need for clarity and consciousness about current reality. The combination of vision and the current reality establishes a particular, very powerful structural tension that is the key to energizing action, maintaining focus, and thus, successfully implementing sustainable development. It will be discussed in chapter 6. Establishing that tension requires that communities next clearly understand the current reality.

HOW DO COMMUNITIES FIND CLARITY ABOUT CURRENT REALITY?

As with the vision and the desired end results, clarity about the current reality requires serious thought and discussion. Enlightened leaders explore it with the community by asking appropriate and probing questions. Relevant current reality for achieving sustainable development goals includes the specifics of the situation relevant to each desired end result, the full range of resources that are in place and available (including efforts), and any actual barriers (not simply hypothetical ones) that have been identified. It may also include very real fears or assumptions about challenges.

Enlightened leaders use open focus practices to guide communities to comprehend an objective, shared view of reality. They don't immediately judge or jump to solutions, recognizing that the current reality must first be seen and understood. They are open to acknowledging what exists, in its entirety, without coloring it or attempting to hide it from others, even if it isn't pretty. They don't shy away from acknowledging problems, situations, or conflicts but examine them deeply, even if they reveal flaws in their own conduct or decisions. They consciously look for biases, ideologies, and beliefs that might color clear understanding, realizing that people often inadvertently or even sometimes deliberately distort reality, relying upon beliefs and ideals that thwart the ability to see what is actually there. Knowing that people are often reluctant to admit they don't know what they don't know and, rather, claim to know what will happen in the future, these leaders identify and acknowledge information gaps. They avoid exaggerating successes or blaming others for lack of results. Also, realizing that because of history or other elements, some communities perceive imaginary barriers, they work to discern whether perceived barriers are real or manufactured or exaggerated. They shine the light on fears and imaginary barriers.

These leaders are open to others' knowledge and understanding of reality. They don't insist that others see things the way they do; they realize that a more complete picture comes as a result of hearing from different people and adjusting the picture to include the most accurate information. They know that, although often ignored by organizations engaged in international development, local knowledge is vital to success.

They use linking communication to assure that information and understanding about current reality are widespread and shared. They demonstrate interest and acceptance of others' views and information, without attachment to their own. They accept that although people will often cling to their impressions, with the right questions, they can expand their understanding. They mentor people to improve their capacity to reach a shared understanding of reality so as to tailor appropriate actions.

Different views and distortions of current reality are the basis for much conflict and stalemate in communities. Enlightened leaders foster collaborative processes to expand understanding of current reality. They know that to assure a shared view, current reality, as much as the vision and desired end results, must be assessed collaboratively. When people have a shared and accurate understanding of reality, they can together develop actions that are logical in light of both the vision and the current state. They can also then use the tension between the two to energize and mobilize action.

To evoke and expand leadership by others, these leaders are continuously alert to and foster contributions by all who show an interest in the community. They guide others in the use of the tools that will help the community move forward. They mentor emerging leaders to expand leadership capacity.

The current situation: Enlightened leaders guide communities to discover the current situation, assets that are already available, and any actual challenges relevant to their desired future by asking questions and then probing more deeply. They first simply ask participants to describe the situation relevant to their desired end result and then ask additional questions to gain the necessary accuracy. To be useful, the description should be quite specific. Fears, doubts, and other emotions can also be part of this description. The main thing is to bring all relevant aspects into the light to reveal logical actions that seem likely to advance the community toward its goals.

The description of the situation should also be described in terms of what exists, not what doesn't. For example: "X amount of funds available," rather than "lack of funds" or "X officials expressing opposition," rather than "lack of official support."

The good: These leaders help communities identify the "good," those resources and assets available to help move toward the goals.

Sometimes, because of habitual thinking, communities first indicate that they have nothing or are helpless. This often results from years of dependency upon government or downplaying available resources, to prove the need for donor assistance. When communities are prompted, however, they usually discover more available resources than they had imagined. For example, leaders can ask what skills, training, or talent people have that can be useful. They can ask what tools are available and what materials they have on hand. Even such things as interest, commitment, and willingness to work can be important resources. Communities, including very poor ones, are often surprised at the resources already available to help them advance toward their goals.

Bad and ugly: "Bad and ugly" aspects of reality refer to actual existing threats and barriers, not simply things people fear might happen. For example, actual legal prohibitions against a particular kind of project would be a negative aspect. A landowner denying access for a necessary road right-of-way or severe subsidence of the roadbed would be other actual barriers to having a good road. Sometimes barriers require accommodation; sometimes they even thwart a goal altogether. More often, they are simply part of reality that must be considered in developing an action plan.

When examined objectively, the current reality grounds the process, to enable the community to take effective action. When reality is distorted, however, it can drastically curtail or derail community progress.

DISTORTIONS OF REALITY

Understanding of reality is often elusive and inaccurate (Fritz 1989, 1996). Some people claim that reality is completely subjective; it is whatever one thinks it is. However, we can know many things objectively, and we can also pinpoint where some aspects are unknown—or even unknowable.

Consciously, or more often unconsciously, people distort reality. Sometimes distortion is deliberate, as when people try to manipulate situations with "fake data" or what is now referred to as "fake news," or when people make unproven assumptions about data. For example, some politicians in the United States claim that crime rates are rising, even astronomically, when data clearly show that although crime rates are high in a few cities, they have steadily declined over several decades in most cities. These same politicians also claim that immigrants are responsible for the majority of the crime, whereas data do not support that claim. Such distortions must be brought into the open and either proven or discounted if communities are to develop actions that are likely to lead to success.

More common, however, is inadvertent distortion, stemming from habitual thought patterns. Identifying some common ones may help to recognize them and to avoid or correct them. By becoming familiar with common distortions, leaders and groups can learn to spot them. Enlightened leaders guide the community to recognize and understand the current reality, whatever it may be. Several forms of distortion are common: (1) making assumptions; (2) vagueness; (3) hiding or ignoring aspects of reality from ourselves or others; (4) exaggerating the negative or the positive; (5) projecting fears into the future, being sure that the worst will happen or that success is impossible; (6) filling the void when reality is unknown. Furthermore, people see reality in different ways; when community members disagree about the current reality, the community cannot move forward in concert.

Assumptions: The most common failure in characterizing current reality accurately is making assumptions about reality. For example, people make assumptions about habits, tendencies, or motivations of other groups, such as those of a different color or sexual orientation, based on a conscious or unconscious bias. Or they make assumptions, based only on guesswork, about what will happen, given the installation of certain laws or policies. When actions are based on an erroneous idea about the reality, actions cannot lead toward a desired future, and massive amounts of resources can be wasted.

Vagueness: People often express the reality in vague and therefore useless terms. *Bad*, *good*, *ugly*, and *failed* are all vague terms that don't say enough about the reality to be useful. Once the detail is fleshed out, the description can be useful. To flesh this out, leaders ask such questions as "If a community wants a thriving economy that provides a good livelihood for everyone, how is the economy now and what opportunities are available to all? If a community wants a new road, does it have a road now? If so, what is the condition of the road? If it wants a school, does it have any school, and if so, what kind of school, relative to the school it wants? If a community has a vision of a clean and green environment, how is the environment now?"

Sometimes, especially if government is involved in a project, community members claim that "the government is corrupt." But what exactly does the word *corrupt* mean in a specific situation? Are high-level officials manipulating contract procedures so as to select their cronies for high-value contracts? Are they in cahoots with underworld figures and then, perhaps, lying about their connections? Are they using illegal means, such as squelching opposition messages or lying about the opposition to influence elections? Are they interfering with media? Are lower-level officials demanding surreptitious payment from someone they accuse of speeding or someone who is trying to obtain a government document? The specifics make a difference in what actions will be appropriate. When participants are specific, they are more likely to find agreement with each other about actual conditions and more able to identify sensible actions.

Ignoring or hiding reality: Sometimes people ignore reality. It may be too painful to face. Sometimes people deny reality, even to themselves, because of what they think it says about them—that they are stupid or incompetent or failures, for example. Some people seem to see every situation through the eyes of what they think it says about them. Enlightened leaders separate themselves from the situation and from what it might say about them and make a concerted effort to see the reality clearly and objectively.

Officials sometimes ignore reality, claiming that a situation is fine, so as to avoid responsibility or expense. For example, drinking water was a bone of contention in Flint, Michigan, where high levels of lead in the water poisoned many children, while officials denied the existence of any problem (Kennedy 2016). If water has a foul taste, people have been sickened after drinking it, or it looks very dirty, the evidence is clear that something is amiss. Testing showed the reality clearly. Had the reality not been denied for so long, fewer children and others would have suffered.

In Brazil, failure to recognize the reality of sand dunes encroaching upon developments (or vice versa) meant millions of dollars wasted on structures continuously overtaken by sand and on futile attempts to bulldoze the sand away.

Exaggerate the negative or the positive: Whether by design or ignorance of the actual reality, exaggeration of the negative or positive are distortions commonly heard from politicians. They may exaggerate the negative, such as when some officials in the United States assert that the existing health-care system will "explode," rather than being specific and accurate about the existing difficulties and addressing them. Or they exaggerate the positive, overblowing the success of their policies to create new jobs, for example, claiming responsibility for the creation of new jobs that had been long planned.

Exaggeration is not limited to officials. Most people do this when imagining, without evidence, a very negative or a very positive future scenario. This generally depends upon a person's life stance or point of view. Some people generally expect bad things to happen. Others have outlawed negative thinking and trained themselves to see only the good. In either case, ignoring the actual reality, whether it is helping to move communities forward or is impeding progress, will limit the community's effectiveness.

Futurecasting: People often make assumptions about what will happen in the future, given certain actions, sometimes based on experience. They might be optimistic or pessimistic. For example, people often assume that things will simply fall into place to lead to their goal. They may assume that others will share their excitement about the proposed new school and willingly donate or budget funds. If they run into roadblocks, which conflict with their distorted view of reality, they may become distraught, engage in blame games, or even give up.

Part of working with current reality is being open to whatever is, and, while keeping the desired end result in mind, seeing what works.

On the pessimistic side, people may assume that achieving a particular goal is hopeless. They may assume that government or others will block their way forward. In one instance, communities were reluctant to discuss their priorities with elected officials, based on their assumptions that the officials wouldn't listen, they didn't care, they already understood the needs, and, in any event, they wouldn't want to help. When these community members investigated, they learned the reality was quite different; the officials helped them in many ways. It might have been otherwise, but they couldn't know until they checked.

People often doubt their ability to achieve a goal. They may believe they are powerless, or that they haven't the right knowledge or skill. These feelings may all be true but often are based on fear and uncertainty, not on reality. Most people don't know what is possible until they try.

The unknowable: Life is full of great mysteries, including why many things happen. Often, events are a result of a combination of apparent coincidences. Because humans are generally uncomfortable with uncertainty, we make up things to fill the void. We often assume we can know the unknowable. We cannot know the future for certain, nor can we know for sure what the result of a certain action will be. The best that can be done is to make educated guesses.

Yet major policy decisions are often made on the back of assertions about the unknowable. Very often, group conflict arises when groups insist they know what the future will bring. At the community level but also at higher levels of government, leaders and citizens get into heated arguments, often without evidence or analysis, about what will happen given a certain economic policy, for example. Some say environmental regulations will kill jobs; others that they will create jobs. Different factions choose evidence to support their claims. Accepting that we don't know and even don't know what we don't know is a powerful realization that can help us stay on track.

Lack of common understanding of reality: Parties may hold differing versions of current reality and the perceived likely future. For example, pro-development groups often declare that negative environmental effects of development are negligible or that they can be prevented, reduced, or combated using technology. Environmental groups often assert that any kind of development in a particular area is disastrous. Lacking a rational approach, clarifying what is known and what is unknown, and coming together around a common understanding of reality, community progress will be stymied. When groups have different views of current reality, they cannot move forward in concert. More effective policies are possible when both proponents and opponents assess the data together after finding clear, shared desired outcomes.

ADDRESSING DISTORTIONS
Distortions of reality must be corrected and reality described accurately to enable people to take sensible actions and to set the dynamic tension that will propel them forward. Enlightened leaders use probing questions and discussion to help communities identify and correct distortions. They do not attempt to correct community

views by simply telling them what reality is. People resist being told that they are wrong.

Questions help communities separate fact from other-than-fact by examining the presence or lack of evidence (Fritz 1996). Leaders can ask if a particular barrier is actually in place or if people are assuming or conjecturing. Are people assuming they can predict the future? The future may or may not resemble the past; people and situations change. If people are denying that any problem exists, objective tests can reveal the facts of the situation.

Leaders may ask questions to reveal the unknown. For example: What is the basis for believing implementation will be easy? For feeling powerless? Have such assumptions been tested? Some aspects of reality are simply unknown at a particular stage; some may never be known.

Without knowing the current reality relative to a community's goals, choosing logical steps to take is impossible. Ignoring this step often leads to a considerable waste of resources or to unexpected outcomes. Establishing and sustaining community focus and moving forward requires that communities have an accurate and shared understanding of the reality, relative to their vision and goals. Enlightened leaders know what questions to ask to help communities clarify reality. They also know and admit when they don't know what they don't know and help communities identify such instances. Helping groups question and understand their own assumptions—including helping them see when they don't and maybe can't know something—is a powerful leadership tool in successful goal implementation.

ALBANIA EXAMPLE

In the CESEDA project, after helping groups identify their priorities and describe their desired end results, coordinators then guided the groups to describe their current reality. This included describing the situations clearly and also describing the assets they had on hand and any real or imagined barriers. They didn't ignore problems, nor did they make them the focus of the process. The villagers at first described the current conditions, relative to the desired result or priority, in vague terms, such as "roads are bad." Coordinators helped them be more specific, using more concrete terms, such as "Particular roads were full of potholes, impassable in rainy weather. Certain schools and clinics were cold and dark, without electricity or heating systems and with ceilings that were falling in."

People were very aware of the conditions, and once they moved past defining everything as simply "bad," they had a picture that was useful in helping them plan appropriate actions.

Villagers identified resources and assets they already had, relative to their desired end results. Although at first they claimed they had nothing of value, they were astonished to see what they had ready and waiting when they inventoried their assets: talents, skills, and experience, as well as physical assets. These included engineers, scientists, teachers, and construction experts and resources such as gravel and other construction materials. They had the foundation for a road or a shell of a school or a clinic, some supplies, and as they soon realized, people who could do the actual labor! They started to see their communities in a new light and started to be better able to consider possibilities that had earlier seemed out of reach. They started to feel more empowered.

Village groups also described any actual (not imagined or feared) roadblocks, such as known political resistance; especially difficult physical constraints of the road, bridge, or school; or other known impediments (fig 5.1).

Figure 5.1. People discuss current reality outside a shop.

People had a widely held distortion of reality that at first got in their way. They resisted talking to officials because they had a preconceived notion that the officials wouldn't listen to them or help them in any way. Coordinators guided them to question their assumptions so as to be more accurate. They asked how they knew what would happen and how they would find out if they didn't make an effort. The coordinators suggested that if the citizens did talk to the officials, they were not guaranteed success, but if they didn't talk to the officials, they were guaranteed failure. When community representatives finally visited the officials and discussed government plans and their own priorities, they were surprised to learn that the officials were quite open and willing to assist with a variety of kinds of assistance. In some cases they actually changed their budget priorities to reflect those of the community and provided full funding;

in other cases they provided technical assistance, equipment, or materials. In some instances, they referred matters that were outside their jurisdiction to the appropriate authorities.

Once the communities understood clearly the full scope of current reality, their actions could be logical, and they could move forward vigorously. Furthermore, as discussed in the next chapter, once they started taking action steps, which included talking with government officials, the community store of resources grew considerably.

Coordinators recorded the information about current reality on the action planning charts, to continue to make the process clear (fig. 5.2). They put the current reality on the bottom of the charts or, when required by the length of the descriptions, made separate pages for the vision and then for the current reality, leaving the "action space" in between. By clarifying the actual conditions, resources, assets, and impediments relevant to the vision, villagers could both celebrate their assets and see more clearly what actions made sense.

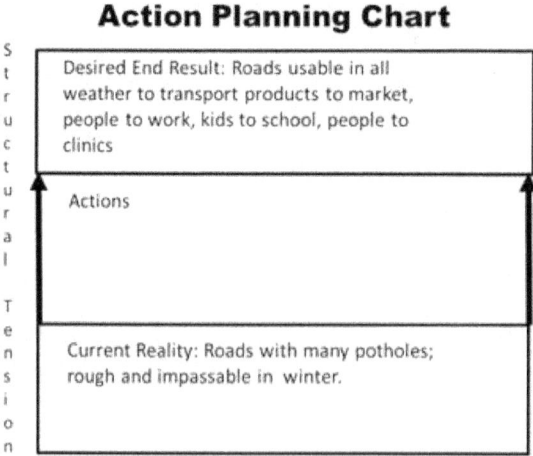

Action Planning Chart

Desired End Result: Roads usable in all weather to transport products to market, people to work, kids to school, people to clinics

Actions

Current Reality: Roads with many potholes; rough and impassable in winter.

Figure 5.2. The second step in the process is recorded on the chart.

Additionally, when they had in their minds both a concrete goal and an accurate picture of the reality, they were energized to move forward and to sustain action. This phenomenon (known in structural dynamics as structural tension) is the key to mobilizing and sustaining community action and progress. Showing this on the charts helped to keep community minds engaged and focused.

SUMMARY AND NEXT STEP

To take appropriate action, communities must know both where they want to go and exactly where they are. Accurately observing what exists helps assure that subsequent actions are well conceived. Since current reality changes over time, communities must track changes and note progress. Although reality often presents unexpected bumps, when communities are clear about what is real, they are able to plan well and keep progressing.

No matter how clear the pictures of the desired end result and the current reality, however, communities would make little progress without action. The third step in this process is to select and take actions that seem likely to advance the community toward the goals. Action steps are the means to the desired ends; as such, they are intended to be experimental. If the project doesn't move forward as anticipated, people can revise the approach, trying different actions. However, the most important key for communities to achieve sustainable development goals successfully is to sustain action over time, even when barriers and distractions arise. Enlightened leaders engage the community spirit to help them take and sustain action and use the dynamics of the structure to advance vigorously.

6

Engaging Community Spirit: Mobilizing Action and Sustaining Progress

The first two implementation steps, engaging community hearts and engaging community minds, are both essential but insufficient. Obviously, communities must take and sustain action if they are to achieve their goals. When the community spirit is engaged—that is, when its essence and unique qualities are appreciated and reflected in its vision for the future—its specific reality is clearly understood, and it is energized; it can then be mobilized. It can move forward with enthusiasm and vigor. This chapter describes the last two steps of the process to implement sustainable development goals: (3) mobilizing action and sustaining progress and (4) completing and celebrating wins.

Successful communities energize and then sustain action using a powerful process based upon principles of structural dynamics (Fritz 1989, 1996). This deceptively simple approach helps people stay focused and moving forward. Sustaining action is the crucial difference between successful implementation and failure; many communities start off with lofty goals and considerable interest and energy, only to wait for others to take the necessary actions. They may be at a loss as to what actions to take. Or they start and then run out of energy before reaching the goals. They sometimes encounter seemingly insurmountable roadblocks and give up. They may get distracted with lesser issues and forget their main aims. People often doubt that the goals can be achieved; most communities have their share of naysayers. However, some of the poorest communities have achieved incredible results against incredible odds and in the face of doubt. No one really knows what they can achieve until they try.

As indicated previously, the process must begin with clarity about both the desired end results and the current reality. When the community has this clarity, it sets in place the energizing and mobilizing tension. The community sustains this tension and action over time by continuously keeping in mind both the desired end result and the current reality to hold the tension.

Enlightened leaders help communities maintain this focus and clarity and keep advancing toward the desired future by continuously engaging community hearts, minds, and spirit. When communities commit to a clearly defined future and at the same time accurately perceive the relevant current reality, they automatically establish a remarkable phenomenon called structural tension (Fritz 1989, 1996). This phenomenon is well known in the arts and sciences. For example, a successful play establishes dramatic tension that must be resolved by the end or leave the audience very dissatisfied. Structural tension is an integral part of structural engineering.

The application of structural tension to community development is, however, relatively unknown. This tension is the engine for forward motion because the natural tendency of structural tension is to seek to resolve. By simply being aware of both their vision and the current reality simultaneously, communities can use this naturally occurring, powerful phenomenon to establish a "path of least resistance," energized by the structural tension, that leads toward their desired future.

Enlightened leaders guide the communities through these next steps of the implementation process, as in the previous ones, using practices of the open focus framework: linking communication, collaborative visioning, and evocative leadership. As with earlier steps, they foster collaboration and consensus in choosing actions, encouraging input from all quarters about what actions should be taken and their subsequent effects. They set up mechanisms to assure expansive two-way communication about the actions and also acknowledge and show support for the participants. They guide the communities to collaborate, together choosing necessary actions to take and evoking the leadership from within the community that will be necessary to see the projects through. They help the communities focus and stay focused on the priority they chose to address.

When communities lose sight of the vision or current reality, as most communities do from time to time, enlightened leaders help them recover the necessary clarity. The chapter describes some of the ways communities lose forward momentum and how enlightened leaders help them reestablish and sustain action to achieve success. It describes how the CESEDA project used these methods to achieve remarkable success.

STEP THREE: MOBILIZING ACTION AND SUSTAINING PROGRESS

Leaders begin this third step in the implementation process by guiding the community to identify a few broad actions that are likely to lead from the current reality to the desired end result or goals. Broad actions will later be broken down into smaller steps. This assures that the plan is logical and doesn't overwhelm people at the outset with excessive detail.

As a means to the desired end results, action steps are intended to be experimental, not set in stone. Actions are tested to see if they do, in fact, lead toward the goals; if not, they can be adjusted. This avoids the waste stemming from a huge effort that ends up heading in the wrong direction.

Each of the broad actions may then be shown at the top of additional, second-level structural- tension charts, with the current status of each indicated at the bottom and the detailed actions that are required and by whom indicated in the center of the chart. This provides a clear, easy-to-follow visual image of where the community is headed, where it is and what it intends to do.

The charts effectively illustrate the difference between the desired future and the current state, reveal what steps may logically lead to the desired future and help focus the community's attention. This is a simple and effective communication tool for keeping the goal clearly in mind and for showing the community's progress. It clearly illustrates the difference between the vision and the reality, helping to motivate continued action. This is similar to the approach often used by community fundraisers who post a thermometer graphic in a public square, showing the goal at the top and the "temperature" steadily moving forward from the starting point, visually representing the difference between the goal and the current reality, which changes over time, and showing the structural tension. However, unlike the thermometer, the chart also shows the action steps.

Enlightened leaders help the community examine the action proposals critically and holistically, with an eye to how the various elements connect. They encourage the community to think through what the intended impacts and unintended consequences are likely to be. Although they cannot predict the future, they know that logical analysis, rather than ideology, can point the way. For example, policies fostering separated land uses not only lead to inefficient use of roads, public transit, and utilities but also spawn automobile dependency, which diminishes walkability and subsequently reduces people's fitness because they walk less. Now, with a surge in interest in walkability, communities are scrambling to retrofit for downtown housing and light-rail systems—but at great cost. Carefully assessing actions helps communities take actions that will lead to their goals, rather than fostering mindless, willy-nilly development.

Taking action, if appropriate to the goal, is itself energizing. As community members see themselves getting closer to their aim, their sense of empowerment and sense of excitement about the desired result generally surges the nearer they come to the vision.

As actions are taken, the current reality will likely change, as the community moves nearer the goal or further away from it. If the current reality does not change in the desired direction, the community can readily see this and try other actions. By constantly keeping the desired end end results and current reality in view, while implementing the action steps, the community sustains the tension and continues to move forward.

However, even very capable and committed communities often start with great enthusiasm, work hard, and then, somewhere along the way, lose momentum and abandon the efforts, perhaps adopting a new endeavor with equal zeal. Skillful enlightened leaders can help them regain their focus and continue moving forward.

GOING OFF TRACK

Unfortunately, communities often fail to achieve their sustainable development goals. Many get off track or give up without reaching their goals. Structural dynamics can usually explain the phenomenon. For various reasons, communities often lose sight of the vision or the current reality and revert to a structure that is not designed for advancement. They find themselves oscillating toward and away from the goals or simply fading out. Some common patterns that lead communities astray are detailed below.

Conflict: A typical pattern of oscillation occurs when various factions refuse to consider shared aims or refuse even to meet with others. This often happens in cases of NIMBY—"not in my backyard"—in which some type of development is proposed for an area, and the neighbors come out in force to block it, without considering how they might work with the proponent to meet the needs of all. Much-needed housing development has been blocked in many areas because of this pattern. When each side is pulling in a different direction, neither can win; they will keep oscillating back and forth.

Sometimes people in divergent factions are convinced that they have nothing in common with other factions, as were businesses and residential neighborhoods in a polarized small city in Colorado where I was facilitating a planning session. When these groups agreed to have a discussion anyway, they discovered that indeed they had the same long-term vision, including a healthy economy and efficient mobility. Once they understood that their disagreement was not about their desired future but about how to achieve it, they were able to focus on that and find ways to accommodate both. Afterward, one of the participants commented: "I didn't think that we [the two groups] could even sit in the same room, much less share the same goals!"

Roadblocks: Sometimes communities have unrealistic expectations about the ease of achieving their goals, and if at first they don't succeed, they simply give up. Those who do succeed use such roadblocks as opportunities to refocus and try again or to try another approach. Just as artists will often keep working on a painting until they achieve the effect they want, communities may need to "create and adjust," trying different things before they achieve the desired future.

Distractions: Oftentimes communities become distracted by lesser goals and forget why they came together in the first place. For example, if a community faces an emergency—which might be man-made, such as an armed conflict, or may be a natural disaster, such as a tornado, a fire, or a flood—it will need to handle the emergency before thinking about sustainable development goals (even though they may be related). This emergency may be so all-consuming that they never get back to the development goals or delay for a very long time.

Sometimes the distractions stem from relatively minor issues as in the aforementioned Colorado sustainability project, when the leadership shifted its focus from its main aim—to promote policies for statewide sustainable development—to how to organize, with different factions pushing for different schemes, until eventually they forgot their major aim.

Lack of commitment: Sometimes communities simply lack a critical mass of people interested enough to take the time and make the effort necessary to move the community forward. Very small groups of two or three people have often achieved impressive results, but without even a small group, progress is unlikely. In Albania, some initially lackadaisical communities in the CESEDA project became motivated when they heard about the results others were achieving; however, a few communities took no action to help their communities. Outside change agents cannot do much to mobilize those who lack desire. Although outside donors may provide improvements, the chance is slight of such communities emerging as vibrant, sustainable communities unless and until they get in touch with a genuinely desired future and then follow through.

Forgetfulness: Sometimes even without any specific distraction, communities forget about their development goals. They may simply become involved in other things, such as day-to-day tasks, and forget about their loftier vision. This happens most commonly when effective leadership is lacking.

All of these situations result from failure to maintain focus on the desired result and an objective view of current reality. Without this focus, the underlying structure is more likely to support a pattern of oscillation rather than a pattern of consistent forward movement.

The remedy is to reestablish the simple structure created by focusing on the vision and the actual current reality to create a path of least resistance that naturally energizes the community's advancement. Leadership is critical.

The enlightened leader who understands the use of structural dynamics and the importance of focus can help the community remember its vision and goals, clearly see current reality (which may change after actions are taken), and then strategize about what actions might be taken next to get back on track and moving forward. *This is the most powerful and effective tool to help communities succeed.*

SUSTAINING PROGRESS

Successful goal achievement requires continuous focus on the desired future and accuracy about current reality. Because of the tendency of communities to sometimes stall or even reverse and fail to progress, the enlightened leader's role is crucial. Enlightened leaders know that the impetus must be sustained by keeping the shared community vision and current reality continuously in mind. If the community loses focus, perhaps diverting to less-important desires or problems and jumping off track, these leaders help to renew the focus and the structural tension. To do so, they track, along with others, the focus on the desired future and progress toward (or regress away from) that desired future. They know that forgetting or misconstruing either the vision or the reality can throw the community off the path and impede or prevent progress.

To assure progress, enlightened leaders ask probing questions, as they did in the beginning, to help people remember and deepen their understanding of both the desired future and the current state (which may have changed) and to evaluate their progress. They may gently remind community members of their vision and current status and events, without blame or criticism, and verify whether they are still committed to a sustainable community future. They show the community how the current situation changes over time.

Enlightened leaders avoid reacting and responding to every problem and issue, knowing that a reactionary approach lessens the likelihood of real progress. At the same time, these leaders acknowledge the reality as it is, including problems, barriers, and distractions, without hiding them from themselves or others. They know that keeping both the vision for the desired future and the current status, relevant to that future, clearly in mind enables the community to choose actions that make sense and to track progress as they experiment. They understand that this is critical for the community to use the powerful structural tension that keeps them moving forward. They also acknowledge and celebrate wins, thus mobilizing further action.

STEP FOUR: COMPLETION AND CELEBRATION

Completion and celebration are two often-overlooked but integral parts of the process to advance toward sustainable development goals. Establishing even a few supportive policies and practices can be fraught with resistance and conflict. In common current political environments, many actors think only about short-term profits or personal rewards. Noting and celebrating progress toward sustainable development acknowledges the community for its commitment and effort and at the same time further energizes it for the next steps. This is especially critical when processes rely extensively upon voluntary action. As one participant said, "When I complete something, it fulfills my soul."

Completion can present challenges. Sometimes community members disagree upon when to call a project complete and move on. Leaders may help to resolve such disputes by guiding discussions to find common ground. Communities also sometimes resist completing a project because completion can leave a void or sense of loss that temporarily halts action. However, having another project ready in the wings can preclude this kind of slump and keep the community energized.

The culmination of this community development process is celebration. This is often forgotten, especially in Western countries in which attention is usually on what is not yet done, on the next goal on the list. Celebration of interim as well as ultimate goals is extremely important to provide closure and an awareness of achievement. It also helps mobilize communities for future projects. Any achievement in the process can be celebrated in any way that people choose and can achieve. The design of celebrations is limited only by the imagination of the planners. For example, if a group has successfully taken a step that has moved the community in the direction of the desired end result, acknowledging that publicly can help maintain the community's sense of achievement and its commitment to keep going. When a major goal is reached, a community-wide celebration brings attention to the capacity and ability of a community to improve and to create a sustainable future. Celebration begets confidence, new aspirations, and a new resolve to tackle still another sustainable development goal.

As indicated previously, celebrations can take many forms, from simply words of praise for a task well done to important in-house ceremonies or community-wide celebrations with food, music, and public speeches. Celebrations sometimes include symbolic elements, which are powerful shorthand reminders of the importance of the community and of people's efforts and express the spirit of the community. For example, the City of San Francisco, California, uses a logo featuring a phoenix, symbolizing the emergence of the City from the ashes of the devastating earthquake and fires of 1906. Similarly, the "reach for the stars" symbol chosen by the City of Prague, Czech Republic, for its proposal to host the 2020 Olympics visually represents the City's aspiration. The range of possible ways communities can choose to celebrate themselves, their aspirations, and their successes is limited only by the imagination of community members. Even if sometimes rudimentary, celebrations confirm and highlight the value of the work a community has done and prompt a renewed focus on continued community improvement. Celebration acknowledges effort and inspires continued success.

CESEDA PROJECT

The CESEDA project in Albania illustrates the last two steps of the implementation process, mobilizing action and sustaining progress and completion and celebration. The initial steps of the process had assured that the spirit of the communities was engaged: community members had described their communities and identified what was important to them; they had themselves decided on their priorities; they understood the current reality, including what resources and assets they had available (fig. 6.1). They were mobilized and ready to move ahead.

Figure 6.1. Community mapping.

In the third step, CESEDA coordinators first asked the communities to define three or four broad actions that seemed likely to move the community situation toward its desired end result. Actions included such things as "discussing the priority with the local government; obtaining supplies; and obtaining resources." They added this information to the action planning charts in the "action space" (fig. 6.2). The charts were a simple but essential tool that helped community members stay focused on the vision, the current reality as it changed over time, and the actions, all at the same time. By showing the basic elements of their plans, they helped to cement and maintain the energizing tension that helps to mobilize and maintain action.

To break down the broad actions to more manageable bits, the charts can then be "telescoped," with each of the major actions shown at the top of a set of second action planning charts, with the current reality relevant to this action step at the bottom and the more detailed action steps indicated in between. As many charts as necessary can be created to show the desired level of detail.

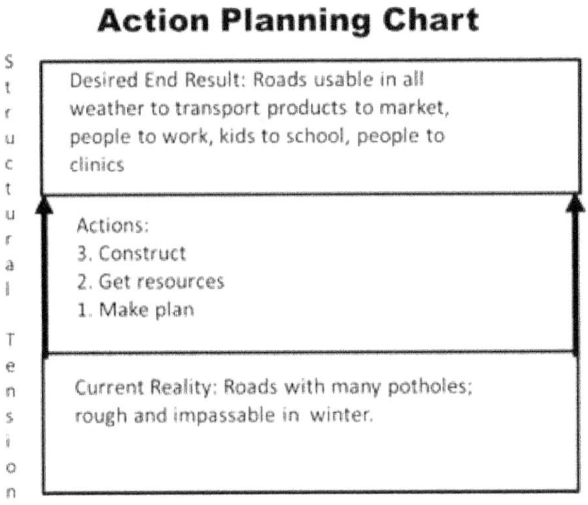

Action Planning Chart

Structural Tension

Desired End Result: Roads usable in all weather to transport products to market, people to work, kids to school, people to clinics
Actions: 3. Construct 2. Get resources 1. Make plan
Current Reality: Roads with many potholes; rough and impassable in winter.

Figure 6.2. Broad actions are shown on the chart; they can be broken into smaller actions and used on additional charts for more detailed planning.

Community Actions: The first part of the process had been relatively easy. The villagers loved doing the "report cards." Evaluating others, without any repercussions, was a rare opportunity. Then, identifying priorities, enabling the communities to select what was most important to them, was also a positive experience. However, when they came to action steps and realized that one essential step was to discuss their priorities with village officials, villagers balked. They explained their reasons: "The officials already know what is needed; the officials won't listen; or, if the officials do listen, they will do nothing."

To help mobilize the communities, the coordinators helped the groups renew the focus on their priorities, assess their own thinking, and explore the accuracy of their view of current reality. They asked such questions as "Can you know for sure in advance what the officials will say? What will be the result if you don't talk with the officials?" Villagers saw that they had nothing to lose but perhaps something to gain (although this was not guaranteed in advance either) by talking with the officials.

Eventually, a few people from each village volunteered to meet with the officials, presenting the report cards that assessed the services and infrastructure and discussing the village priorities. They asked the officials if the local government had any plans to address these priorities. With this non-threatening and collaborative approach (not a confrontational one), much to the surprise of the villagers, the officials generally responded positively, agreeing to help in various ways (fig. 6.3).

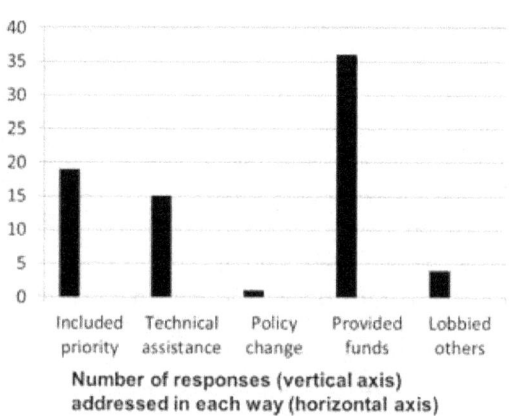

Figure 6.3. Local officials responded positively to 52 % of village priorities.

In some cases, the officials already had a plan to address the priority; in others, they adjusted their budgets to reflect the priority of the village. They forwarded some priorities, such as those addressing schools or medical facilities, to regional offices of the central government or to specific units of the local or regional government. If local governments lacked the resources to conduct or fund a project fully, they usually provided professional expertise, supplies, and/or loaned equipment. Villager volunteers usually contributed the labor; they sometimes also contributed money and supplies. The officials' response demonstrated the inaccuracy of initial assumptions and helped participants become more accurate about the reality.

Although villagers were even more reluctant to meet with central government officials than with local ones, eventually several volunteers came forward. They attended meetings with ministry officials, describing their major shared priorities among the villages. As a result, some village priorities became part of the National Strategy for Social and Economic Development.

As a result of these meetings, the communities obtained equipment, supplies, and resources, which they supplemented with donations from other individuals and groups, including a few small grants from CESEDA, and their own contributions. When they had what they needed, remarkably, community members, new to both collaboration and self-help, did most of the work building and rebuilding. As a result, fifty villages completed fifty-eight significant improvement projects such as roads, schools, health centers, sewage removal, and water projects (fig. 6.4; 6.5, 6.5.).

Figure 6.4. New Bridge in Baldushk

Figure 6.5. Villagers Improve Road in Petrele

Figure 6.6. Public Private Partnership

Did this process succeed in every instance? No, some of the village groups, usually more remote ones, never came together and never took action. Attitudes and practices of officials, donors, and implementers also presented some challenges, however well-intentioned these groups were. Some local officials resisted input from the people. They were considered to be, after all, the experts who knew what the communities needed, what was possible, and how to provide it. Village leaders were unaccustomed and resistant to sharing power in decision making. Likewise, donors and implementers sometimes thought they knew best what the villages needed and what they could do—and they underestimated the ability of the villagers.

Completion and Celebration: CESEDA guided the initiation of community festivals such as those held in many other countries, to celebrate each community's achievements and their local resources and also offer family entertainment. Sometimes the results were not quite those envisioned by staff. For example, one such festival focused on turkeys, the pride of a particular village, which were generally taken to the market in the capital city of Tirana to sell only for New Year's celebrations. Although staff attempted to persuade the village to conduct the festival before Christmas, when many expat residents would be seeking turkeys, the village held it on December 26. On that day, when staff rounded the hill to see the festival below, about fifty men were standing around, about two hundred turkeys were tethered to the ground, one table held a few jars of honey, and a big homemade sign advertised that the festival was sponsored by USAID (fig. 6.7). Not a woman was in sight. It was clearly not the kind of festival that staff had imagined.

Figure 6.7. Village Turkey Festival.

However, this festival was a success in that many people came to buy turkeys. More importantly, the festival was a success because it belonged to the community. They had created something they wanted and liked. The community continued the turkey festival in subsequent years, thus lifting the burden of transporting their turkeys to the central market. The experience reiterated the importance of engaging the community hearts, minds, and spirit, enabling the residents to create what they wanted, rather than to implement what others thought was appropriate.

In Albania, overcoming historical and cultural constraints and changing behavior to achieve community goals took time, patience, and experience. Nevertheless, for fifty villages in Albania, with their background, to complete fifty-eight significant projects was extraordinary. Even more important than completion of the individual projects, however, was the change in the awareness and capacity of the participants, "changing the mentality," as local staff had suggested. By employing practices of the open focus framework and principles of structural dynamics in the implementation steps, the villagers developed the power and ability to continue to make positive changes in their communities.

CESEDA participants continued to use the approach and tools long after project completion. The action planning framework provided a visual focus to help them both identify logical actions and stay focused on their aim. They saw that they could work with each other and with government. They had discovered that by working together, advocating for and planning and taking action toward their own priorities, they could do much to improve their communities. At the same time, government, especially local government, learned to pay more attention to the needs and preferences expressed by local communities and eventually to seek input from them (fig. 6.8).

Figure 6.8. Meeting with local official.

SUMMARY AND NEXT STEPS

This chapter has described how leaders guide communities in the third step of the implementation process—to mobilize action and sustain progress toward the goals. At the core of success are the practices of an open focus framework: linking communication, collaborative vision, and evocative leadership, which enable leaders to guide communities effectively. When communities take action and experience success, they become even more energized and more convinced of their ability to advance toward their goals. The chapter has also shown the utility of specifically completing and celebrating results, the fourth step in the process. People benefit from a sense of completion and being acknowledged and rewarded for their efforts and achievements.

Enlightened leaders understand and include celebration to knowledge success, to stimulate further action, and to evoke new leadership. When a group has successfully taken a step that moved the community closer to a goal, acknowledging that publicly can arouse the community's sense of achievement and its commitment to continue. When a major goal is achieved, a community-wide celebration brings attention to the capacity and ability of a community to improve its own status and to create a sustainable future. Whatever the form of a celebration, it will help to foster pride, confidence, and renewed focus on the community and its development and resolve to tackle still another community goal.

This framework (fig. 6.7) is designed and has been proven to enhance significantly the success of efforts to achieve sustainable development goals. The various elements work together to aid any leaders including those in sponsor and donor organizations, implementing agencies, academic institutions, and communities who strive to achieve this most critical and timely aim.

IMPLEMENTATION FRAMEWORK FOR SUSTAINABLE DEVELOPMENT

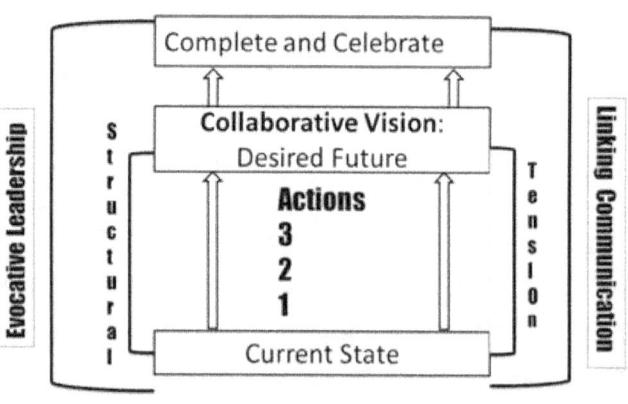

Figure 6.7. Enlightened leaders use tools of the open focus framework and structural dynamics to achieve sustainable development goals.

The final chapter will describe some next steps that international organizations, government agencies, donors, NGOs, practitioners, educators, local leaders, and all others who design, sponsor, and guide sustainable development efforts can take to help communities achieve greater success in the twin aims of accomplishing sustainable development goals and combating global climate change.

7

Accelerating Progress to a Sustainable Future

Previous chapters have described how open focus leadership and principles of structural dynamics influence implementation of efforts to combat global climate change and advance sustainable development goals. Focusing on communities, the locus of most sustainable development activities, we explained how and why a commonly used problem-focused approach fails to move communities forward and how progress is often thwarted or reversed because of the underlying foundation that guides action. We showed how focusing on problems leads in a circular pattern and how groups working at odds or on conflicting goals are destined to oscillate ad infinitum. We showed how, in contrast, when communities come together around a shared vision for the future that engages their hearts, minds, and spirit and at the same time have a shared understanding of the current reality, the resulting structural tension mobilizes action and advances progress.

The complexity of the community demands special leadership tools and approaches. Most importantly, the life-threatening and complex nature of global climate change and the essential need for sustainable development demand use of the most effective leadership tools and approaches available. We illustrated how enlightened leaders use an open focus framework including the tools of linking communication, collaborative envisioning, and evocative leadership to engage hearts, minds, and spirit of communities to inspire, energize, and mobilize the enthusiastic and sustained involvement of community members. Organizations sponsoring, funding, and guiding projects, along with local community leaders, can significantly improve success in combating climate change and achieving sustainable development goals using this approach.

SUSTAINABLE COMMUNITY DEVELOPMENT CASES

Although myriad accounts of the successful use of this approach by individual organizations have been documented, only a few cases of its application to the complex community structure have been documented. The following are some of them.

As discussed earlier, the process has been the heart of the community building for more than twenty-five years in one of the first projects to use it, the Uganda Rural Development Training Programme, which has empowered tens of thousands of people to create a vision of what they want in their lives and to work together to achieve that vision (Fritz 2015; Seybold 2013). Using the creative process and structural dynamics, they have improved the quality of their lives and the prosperity of their homes and their communities.

Also discussed previously was the 1995 Sustainable Forestry and Agriculture Project in Vietnam, which used this process in its work with four provinces and dozens of villages. By guiding the communities to discover their visions and desired end results and to understand the reality clearly, they established an underlying foundation designed for progress. Project facilitators helped the villages mobilize and keep advancing toward their sustainable development goals.

In the tiny, impoverished community of Los Ojos in the State of New Mexico, a small group of committed leaders fostered sustainable community development that relied upon high-quality merino sheep wool, organic meat, and talented weavers (Sargent et al. 1991). They started with both a clear vision of a desired future and a clear picture of the actual starting conditions, establishing a structure that led to several lucrative and successful enterprises that revitalized the community and provided a livelihood for many residents, while maintaining cultural, social, and environmental health.

In a remote Appalachian region, Dr. Alta Schrock mobilized dozens of people to create many avenues for sustainable social and economic development, providing jobs and income and revitalizing communities. An inspiring vision, shared by many, coupled with a keen awareness of the relevant current conditions, was the starting point for the enormous strides made in the region (Coe 1993).

In Albania, the CESEDA project demonstrated how leaders applied tools of an open focus approach to the four implementation steps to help fifty communities complete fifty-eight significant social and economic improvements in their communities and then to continue using the approach to make even more improvements (Coe 2013).

ROLE OF ENLIGHTENED LEADERS

Leaders who understand the basics of this approach make an enormous difference in guiding communities to enhance development endeavors. Using an open focus approach, they use linking communication to establish workable communication links to assure widespread knowledge and understanding of the effort and show how to communicate clearly and supportively, rather than defensively. They demonstrate the process of working collaboratively with others, being open to the views and preferences of all. They guide communities to discover a shared and inspiring desired future and to hold an accurate picture of the relevant current reality. They show how to experiment with action—trying things, evaluating, and then adjusting when needed. These leaders then show how the structural tension helps to mobilize and sustain action and progress. They convey the importance of maintaining focus on the vision and reality, recognizing that the capacity for clarity is one of the most important facets of successful goal implementation. They guide the communities in the use of the naturally occurring phenomenon to establish a path of least resistance that leads toward their desired future.

These leaders also evoke the leadership of others and provide formal or informal training and mentoring in techniques of open focus leadership and the steps of the implementation process. Leadership expands geometrically; as new leaders emerge, those leaders, in turn, are inspired to pass it along.

Most importantly, being acutely aware that sustainable community development requires a long-term focus on the desired future and sustained activity toward it, these leaders show how to maintain or renew the structure necessary for success. They understand how forgetting or misconstruing either the vision or the reality can throw the community off the path and impede or prevent progress. If the community loses focus, perhaps diverting to less-important desires or problems and jumping off track, they gently help communities revisit their vision and current reality and reestablish structural tension. They may ask probing questions to help people remember and deepen their understanding of both the desired future and the current state and to evaluate their progress. They also teach others how to focus on the desired future and sustain progress when tempted to react to circumstances and problems and forget their aspirations. In this way, they help communities maintain the structural tension that energizes and sustains progress.

They also acknowledge and celebrate wins, thus stimulating further action. When the community achieves interim or end results, they guide the community to recognize and acknowledge the achievement and to celebrate.

WHAT'S NEXT?

Research and practice have demonstrated that this approach can significantly improve implementation of sustainable development goals and efforts to combat global climate change. Its efficacy has been seen in such diverse countries as Albania, Uganda, and Vietnam. Now the critical question is, how can this understanding be disseminated and used by those who are responsible for assuring a future that supports the needs and goals of people worldwide? It can be applied in many more communities to improve significantly the implementation of sustainable development goals. Additional research and development and documentation of additional cases can help assure that climate change and sustainable development efforts benefit from the knowledge gained thus far by organizations and development projects using the approach.

International organizations such as the United Nations Development Programme (UNDP), World Bank, Organization for Security and Cooperation in Europe, World Vision, World Learning for International Development; individual country programs such as the United Kingdom Department for International Development (DFID), the US Agency for International Development (USAID), Canadian International Development Agency (CIDA), Swedish International Development Agency (SIDA); and private foundations such as the Ford Foundation, Rockefeller Foundation, or others could achieve greater success from their efforts to combat global climate change and achieve sustainable development goals using this process in designing and sponsoring projects and programs. They would also be logical sponsors for demonstration and evaluation projects.

A useful next step would be to conduct action research projects in a variety of communities and contexts. Expansion to additional communities in a few different countries, with concise evaluation and documentation, can assure that the methodology is consistent and can expand knowledge of how best to use the process. It can show what barriers may need to be addressed and overcome and how the process may be made more efficient and even more effective. Demonstration and evaluation projects would involve structuring projects in several communities in different but diverse less-developed or transitional countries that are relatively stable but in need of improvement in many realms to become environmentally, economically, and socially sustainable. Ideally, these projects would be conducted on several different continents. As in Albania, the project would involve teaching the methodology to project coordinators and facilitators, who would then work with local communities. The projects would include a system for evaluation established at the outset. The projects would take place simultaneously, and then the results would be compared across project sites, to identify commonalities and differences.

I hope that this book has challenged readers to be open to innovative and potentially results-changing ideas and that it can stimulate more effective approaches to what have been intractable challenges. If sustainable development goals are to be achieved and achieved in a timely fashion, a drastic change in approach is necessary. Open focus leadership, grounded in structural dynamics, can profoundly enhance the success of all those attempting to implement sustainable development goals and combat global climate change.

References

Barker, Joel. 1985. "The Power of Vision." *Discovering the Future Series* (videotape). Burnsville, MN: Charthouse International.

Bloomberg, Michael R. 2017. Interview, *Charlie Rose Show*, PBS, aired April 24.

Braga, Ricardo Burgo. 2015. Unpublished manuscript.

Coe, Barbara A. 2013. "Linking Communities and Government for Social and Economic Development: How Villagers in Albania Worked with Government to Change Minds and Improve Conditions." *Journal of the Public Administration Academy* (Yerevan, Armenia): 39--9.

_____. 2008. "Engaging Communities: Albania as an Example." *Public Administration Times* 1 (32): 5.

_____. 2001. "Strategic Planning for Healthy Communities." In *Citizen Participation Handbook*, edited by Gina Galbreath

Holdar and Olha Zakharchenko, 39–46. People's Voice Project, International Centre for Policy Studies. Kyiv, Ukraine: iMedia.

_____.1997. "How Structural Conflicts Stymie Reinvention." *Public Administration Review* 57 (2): 168–73.

_____.1995. Personal observation and participation.

_____.1993. "Women Leaders in Community Development: Alta Schrock, Pathfinder, Bridgebuilder." Presentation, Annual Conference of the International Society for Community Development, Milwaukee, WI, July.

_____.1991. "Open Focus: A Community Development Model." *Journal of the Community Development Society* 21 (2): 18–35.

_____.1988. "Open Focus: Implementing Projects in Multi-Organizational Settings." *International Journal of Public Administration* 11 (4): 503–26.

_____.1987. "An Open Focus Framework for Strategic Plan Implementation in Public-Private Partnerships." *Western Governmental Researcher* 3 (1): 49–62.

_____.1986. An Open Focus Framework For Goal Implementation in Public-Private Partnerships. Ann Arbor, Michigan: Dissertation Information Service.

Cohen, Michael D, James G. March, and Johan P. Olsen, 1972. "A Garbage Can Model of Organizational Choice." *Administrative Science Quarterly* 17 (1): 1–25.

Eisenstein, Charles. 2013. *The More Beautiful World Our Hearts Know Is Possible*. Berkeley: North Atlantic Books.

EU Commission. 2017. "Climate Action." https://ec.europa.eu/clima/policies/international/negotiations/paris_en.

Fritz, Robert. 2015. Robert Fritz Inc. "One of the world's best development programs." https://www.robertfritz.com/wp/one-of-the-worlds-best-development-programs/.

_____. 1996. *Corporate Tides: The Inescapable Laws of Organizational Structure*. San Francisco: Berrett-Koehler.

_____.1989. *The Path of Least Resistance: Learning to Become the Predominant Creative Force in Your Own Life*. Revised edition. New York: Random House.

Goodall, Jane. 2017. Interview on the *Charlie Rose Show*, PBS, aired April 13.

Gruber, N.L.S., Strohaecker, T.M, Ayup-Zouain Y R.N. Y Farina, F. 2011. *Subsídios à Gestão Costeira: vulnerabilidades ambientais e aspectos legais para normativas de uso e ocupação. In:* López, R.A., Marcomini, S.C (Eds). (ISBN 978-987-1527-24-3) Problemática de los Ambientes Costeros, Sur de Brasil, Uruguay y Argentina p.41-57.

International Fund for Agricultural Development, Republic of Albania. 2002. "Country Strategic Opportunities Paper." http://www.ifad.org/gbdocs/eb/84/e/EB-2005-84-R-8.pdf.

Kennedy, Merrit. 2016. "Lead-Laced Water in Flint: A Step-by-Step Look at the Makings of a Crisis." Spokane Public Radio, April 20. http://www.npr.org/sections/thetwo-way/2016/04/20/465545378/lead-laced-water-in-flint-a-step-by-step-look-at-the-makings-of-a-crisis.

Kretzmann, John P., and John L. McKnight. 1993. *Building Communities from the Inside Out: A Path Toward Finding and Mobilizing a Community's Assets.* Evanston, IL: Institute for Policy Research.

Mumo, Michael. 2016. "Political Will Key in Successful Implementation of SDGs." *Capital News*, September 22. http://www.capitalfm.co.ke/news/2016/09/political-will-key-successful-implementation-sdgs-expert/.

Phillips, Noelle. 2016. "Homicides in Denver hit 9-year high with 50 people killed in 2015." *Denver Post*, January 17. http://extras.denverpost.com/homicides/2015/.

Sargent, Frederic O., Paul Lusk, Jose A. Rivera, and Maria Varela. 1991. "Sustainable Development: Ganados del Valle Enterprises." In *Rural Environmental Planning for Sustainable Communities*, 196–212. Washington, DC: Island Press.

Senge, Peter. 2008. *The Necessary Revolution: How Individuals and Organizations Are Working Together to Create a Sustainable World.* New York: Doubleday.

Seybold, Patricia. 2013. "How Uganda Rural Development Training Programme (URDT) and the African Rural University (ARU) are *already* meeting the Engelbart Challenge." Patricia Seybold Group.

https://collectiveiq.wordpress.com/2013/12/13/how-these-rural-initiatives-in-uganda-are-already-meeting-the-engelbart-challenge/ Thankyouocean.org. 2017. "Marine Protected Areas." http://thankyouocean.org/threats/marine-protected-areas/.

United Nations Development Programme. "Sustainable Development Goals." 1 January 2016, the 17 Sustainable Development Goals (SDGs) of the 2030 Agenda for Sustainable Development. http://www.undp.org/content/undp/en/home/sustainable-development-goals.html.

URDT. 2017. Uganda Rural Development Training Programme 2017. http://www.urdt.net/index.php/awards.html.

www.ingramcontent.com/pod-product-compliance
Lightning Source LLC
Chambersburg PA
CBHW071410280526
45787CB00001B/502